Human Societies

natalienguyen

Human Societies

an introduction

Abram de Swaan

translated by Beverley Jackson

Polity

Copyright © Abram de Swaan 2001

The right of Abram de Swaan to be identified as author of this work has been asserted in accordance with the Copyright, Designs and Patents Act 1988.

First published in 2001 by Polity Press in association with Blackwell Publishers Ltd

Editorial office:
Polity Press
65 Bridge Street
Cambridge CB2 1UR, UK

Marketing and production:
Blackwell Publishers Ltd
108 Cowley Road
Oxford OX4 1JF, UK

Published in the USA by
Blackwell Publishers Inc.
350 Main Street
Malden, MA 02148, USA

A catalogue record for this book is available from the British Library.

Library of Congress Cataloging-in-Publication Data
Swaan, A. de.
 [Mensenmaatschappij. English]
 Human societies : an introduction / Abram de Swaan ; translated by Beverley Jackson.
  p. cm.
Includes biblographical references and index.
 ISBN 0-7456-2591-6 (hard : alk. paper)—ISBN 0-7456-2592-4 (pbk. : alk. paper)
 1. Social systems. 2. Social interaction. I. Title.
 HM701 .S913 2001
 301—dc21
                              00-010177

Typeset in 11 on 13 pt Sabon
by SetSystems Ltd, Saffron Walden, Essex

This book is printed on acid-free paper.

Contents

Contents

Contents

Foreword

This is a brief and elementary introduction to the science of society. It may be read without any prior schooling in the social sciences, but readers will need some experience and knowledge of social life to complement the discussions in this book with their own examples and counter-examples. Less experienced readers may use it as a textbook in an introductory social science course.

Human Societies offers a broad review of the core insights achieved by the social sciences. The subject-matter is presented in a common framework, without much regard for the borders between anthropology, sociology or political science, or the dividing lines between area specialisms and schools of thought, while the academic debates on the true meaning of concepts and the real intentions of the founders are largely ignored. This is a book about social life, not about the social sciences. The fundamental ideas from those disciplines can stand on their own, independently of their social and intellectual origins.

The book's content and structure are based on historical sociology in the broad sense – as the most general science of society. This leads to a strictly systematic presentation of the subject matter that will help readers to order their own thoughts and experiences. Each chapter addresses a fundamental question about people in their various arrangements. The first is: what do people need from one another; what do they need to survive and how do these needs make them dependent upon others? Subsequent chapters deal with the ties that bind people, the expectations they entertain of one another, their means of distinguishing themselves from others, the ways they have of moulding and teaching the young, and what they believe, know and invent. The remaining chapters of the book discuss the ways in which people coordinate their activities so as to constitute social arrangements: these range from foraging bands of only a few dozen members to contemporary societies that can coordinate a billion people or more quite effectively. This hundred-millionfold increase in the scale of social life occurred in the brief course of five to ten thousand years, as new forms of human coordination emerged: from reciprocal obligation, collective action, to markets, organizations and states, and finally, the emerging global level of interdependence and coordination.

In the course of dealing with the chapter topics, the core concepts and ideas of the social sciences are introduced whenever they may serve the readers to understand the social processes in which they themselves are also involved: role conflict, status convergence, self-fulfilling prophecy, socialization, stratification, division of labour and so on. The connection with social science literature is made in the bibliographical notes at the end of the book: for each chapter there is a list of titles, each with a very brief description, for those who want to read on. This, I trust, will make up for the fact that I took much from these books without mentioning them in the main text. It is also meant as a tribute to the authors whose work I read with so much pleasure and profit. I hope the readers will derive as much benefit from these titles as I did.

I began this introductory text in 1976 as a visiting professor at the University of Surinam, just after the country gained its independence. I continued to work on it for almost twenty-five years, while students constantly provided criticism and comments, forcing me to repeat the material and reformulate it, hopefully in better words each time. Often they would understand something other than what I had intended, sometimes having understood my meaning very well. This book is dedicated to all those objecting, dissenting and understanding students. But I had other readers as well. I worked long and hard with Theo van Praag and Dries van Ingen to revise the text. In the Amsterdam School for Social Science Research the book was discussed at length by the participants in the seminar 'A social science for beginners for advanced students'. In the final stages I received plenty of good advice from Kitty Roukens, Hans Sonneveld, Johan Goudsblom and the editors of the Dutch publisher, Bert Bakker. Robert van Krieken, Stephen Mennell and the staff at Polity were most helpful in preparing this English edition. They made this a better book. But for the time being, this is the definitive version.

Abram de Swaan

1

What People Need from One Another

People need other people for every aspect of their lives. They are conceived through other people and they are *dependent* on others for their survival. Everything that they need but cannot make themselves must come from others. What they need to know and do not know yet must be learnt from others. People cannot do without each other. That is why they live together in large or small *social arrangements*: small family units or extended families, villages, neighbourhoods, societies and businesses, churches, unions and political parties, groups of friends and classes at school. The most comprehensive social arrangement is referred to simply as *society*.

1 People as interdependent beings

No one lives completely separately from other human beings. Even the hunter who roams the forest carries tools that someone else has made. At the end of the hunt he returns to the inhabited world and sells the hides of the animals he has shot or trapped to buyers, so as to be able to purchase all sorts of things that are unobtainable in the forest.

For it is impossible to make everything you need yourself, and everyone is therefore reliant on the products of others. Even something as simple as a hunting knife takes dozens of people to make it: someone to mine the ore, someone to melt

1

down the iron ore into iron, someone to harden the steel and someone to forge the blade. And each of these people in turn needs tools and raw materials that others have made.

All these activities must be geared to one another, so that one person can go on working with the products that someone else has supplied. So a knife, or any product at all, embodies the concerted efforts of an entire *network* of people.

Similarly, no one can work out every problem unaided, or see beforehand all the knowledge and skills that will be needed in order to survive in the world. So every individual relies on fellow human beings to pass on this necessary knowledge and these essential skills. Children do not learn to speak automatically – they pick it up from their parents, and their brothers and sisters. Nor do toddlers automatically know what is good for them. They put all sorts of things in their mouths, and it takes them a long time to register what they are told – that some things are 'edible' and others 'dirty' or 'poisonous', that food may be 'clean' or 'unclean'.

Small children are dependent on others to take care of them, and a baby which is left to fend for itself will not survive for very long. In the event of illness or accident, and in old age, we are dependent on others to take care of us. When people are described as 'independent', it does not mean that they do not need anyone else; it means that they can pay for everything that is done for them, either with money or by doing something else in return. No one is independent. People cannot take care of themselves; at most they can ensure that others will take care of them.

These mutual dependencies mean that people are linked to one another. *Social arrangements consist of people who are connected by mutual dependencies.* In other words, social arrangements consist of *interdependent* people.

Social science studies people in the social arrangements they form with one another. That is what this book is about: about the origins and the workings of social arrangements, and about the changing patterns of dependence between people.

2 Conditions for human survival

What do people need in order to survive, and what do they need their fellow human beings for? To put it differently, what *conditions* are necessary for human existence? Certain conditions apply to almost all living creatures: they must have access to sufficient (but not too much) oxygen, the air temperature must not be too high or too low, and so forth. Physical conditions like these will not concern us here. We are concerned with conditions that make people dependent upon their fellow human beings, i.e. *social conditions for existence*:

1 All people need *food* every day;
2 They need *shelter*;
3 They need *protection* from enemies and predatory animals;
4 They need the *affection* of others;
5 They cannot do without *knowledge* about the surrounding world;
6 They must be able to *control* themselves.

The list could be extended and elaborated. But it sums up the main conditions that must be fulfilled for people to survive. How they are fulfilled, however, will differ enormously from one society to the next.

As long as the conditions for their existence are met, people scarcely stop to think about them. It is only when something is lacking, or when some threat is perceived, that they become aware of them: then they experience a *need* for food, for protection, or for affection. Although the conditions for existence are roughly the same for all people, the way in which people experience their needs may be very different.

People are dependent on others because they can only fulfil the necessary conditions for their continued existence together with other people. The ways in which they do so reflect the kinds of social arrangements they form with one another.

Food

Nowadays, even those people who do possess a garden are more likely to plant flowers in it than they are to grow potatoes or grain. Some families do keep a little plot of land to grow some of their own food. In general, however, people buy their food washed and weighed, processed and packaged in the shops, and sometimes they even have it served up to them in a restaurant. Even farmers, who certainly produce food on a large scale, eat very little of their produce themselves. They sell most of the harvest, and use the money – just like anyone else – to do their shopping at the butcher's, the baker's and the greengrocer's. While modern farmers tend to produce a great deal, they produce a great deal of the same thing; for a varied diet they purchase their food elsewhere.

In a modern society, then, people are completely dependent on others for their food: dependent on shopkeepers, who in turn rely on auctioneers and wholesalers, who obtain their wares from growers, manufacturers and importers. Thus, everyone is dependent on others for their food supply, but not on any one particular individual, for buyers can always decide to take their trade elsewhere. Nowadays, there are fewer and fewer farmers producing the food for the rest of the population, who do not themselves produce food but are occupied with other things. Less than a hundred years ago, almost one-third of the working population of Europe was engaged in agriculture or fishing; now the figure is under 5 per cent. And it was only a few decades ago that many factory workers had vegetable gardens at home, and kept chickens, rabbits or a goat. So their families were partly self-sufficient for their food, rather than being totally dependent on shopkeepers.

In traditional agriculture, a farmer's family lived almost entirely off the land, and had little left to exchange or sell. This is still the normal pattern of life for the rural population in large parts of the world: farming families that eat everything they grow and grow everything they eat. These households, as they meet their food requirements themselves, are not – for their food – dependent on others. But it follows that the individual members of such a family are all the more dependent on each other: to work the land, to fetch in the harvest, to care for the animals and to prepare the food. The small children are dependent on their parents, and the grandparents on their children. (This is why people in such countries often want to have large families, to ensure that they will be cared for in their old age.) Such farming families are therefore extremely dependent on just a few people – their relatives.

Since the variety of food available has also increased, people can make choices and develop their own taste and style. This gives rise to wider variations between people within a society, and individuals can adopt distinctive styles of eating.

The pattern of dependence within a society apparently changes to reflect the way in which the food supply is arranged. The *network of dependencies* surrounding the food supply stretches much further in present-day society, and connects far more people than before, at every intersection.

Shelter

People must be able to protect themselves from heat and cold, from wind and rain, and from vermin. This they do in two ways: with clothing (which they carry about with them on their bodies) and with a dwelling (which generally remains in one place). In some regions people cannot go a single day without clothes or a roof over their heads, while in others people scarcely need such protection at all. This obviously has to do with the climate and season.

Spinning, weaving and sewing were all traditionally women's work, which meant that men and children were dependent on women for their clothing. The material was made from sheep's wool, cotton or flax. So farming families could take care of these needs themselves. But when it came to dwellings, stables and sheds, things were generally tackled differently in traditional agricultural societies. To put up these buildings and structures required the help of neighbours. The assistance would be repaid when the neighbours in turn needed a new house to be built. This repayment in kind, or *mutual assistance*, linked together households that were fairly independent for their food supply in a larger network of dependencies. People who had exerted themselves for their neighbours had to hope and trust that these neighbours would fulfil their obligations when it was their turn to do so.

Nowadays, very few people build their own houses. Other people are always needed for this task, but neighbours no longer enter into the picture. Houses are designed by architects and built under the supervision of building contractors by bricklayers, carpenters, electricians and plumbers – in short, by skilled workers who have made this skill into their paid occupation. The houses they build are offered to others for sale or for rent. The builders do not work because they must return a service to someone; usually, they do not even know who will be living in the new house. They work because they receive wages in the form of money, which they can use to buy food and clothing and to rent or buy a house of their own. This is how a *money economy* works. Because people all apply themselves to a particular type of work or product, which they supply indirectly to others for money, people do not have to use everything they make; by the same token, they can use things without having to make them. The money they receive for their own products can be used to purchase the products of others. So the work to be done is divided up among countless specialists: this is the *division of labour* in society. The division of labour and the money economy make it possible to use things without producing them oneself, and they also make it necessary for everyone to produce something – not for the purpose of using it, but in order to gain money to buy other people's products. This extends the network of dependencies still further: as far as the money goes.

Protection

People may find their existence threatened from various sources, not only by a shortage of food, by cold weather or storms, but also by germs, predators and other people. For most modern people, lions and tigers are attractions to be viewed at the zoo or on safari, but once they constituted a direct threat. Only a hundred years ago, wolves and bears regularly claimed victims in sparsely populated areas of Europe and America, and tigers are feared even today in the peasant villages of South Asia. In prehistoric times, the hunting of large wild animals was in effect a war waged by people against other animal species. To track down those animals and kill them, the hunters had to be able to rely on one another and to harmonize their actions with great precision: *coordination* was essential. And after the hunt, they had to agree about how to divide up the spoils. But many tens of thousands of years ago, humans triumphed over other species in the fight for existence, driving the large predators into inaccessible corners of the world. Most of these species are now even threatened with extinction by humans.

Since that battle was won, the greatest threat to people has come from two sides: from germs, which can cause disease, and from other people, who may try to take some-one else's life or property. For protection against germs, people are nowadays dependent on medical practitioners. And for protection from robbers or enemy soldiers they also rely on their fellow human beings: to ward off armed robbers and assailants they need armed guards or police, and to repel enemy forces they need forces of their own.

When people first settled in one place to work the land, they became especially vulnerable to attack by other people looking for a chance to plunder the crops in their fields, their cattle or their stores. In general, the more productive a society is, the more vulnerable it becomes. Many peoples abandoned agriculture – or even decided not to try it – because they knew the yield would arouse the envy of pillaging neighbours. One band of warriors would drive out another to claim the spoils for itself. In the course of time, this band ceased to plunder at random; instead it would impose a fixed duty on the peasants in the area – a tribute – and keep other marauders away. In this way, the peasants and the warriors became dependent on one another for tribute and protection.

So relationships of dependence do not only arise when people cooperate in some way; they will often develop between two groups both living in conflict with a third group. These dependence networks based on tribute and protection grew into military-agricultural societies covering vast areas and containing many hundreds of thousands of people.

Affection

People are also unable to do without the affection and regard of their fellow human beings. Very small children who are given enough to eat and drink and are laid in their cots covered with warm blankets can nevertheless be stunted in their development or become ill if there is no one to cuddle them and play with them. Experiments are not conducted with human babies, but there have been studies of the inmates of children's homes who were fed and changed but not cuddled or spoken to. These children became 'institutionalized'. They failed to develop properly, proved little resistant to disease, became despondent and apathetic, and lost all interest in their surroundings. That children – and adults too – need love and friendship from others is something that everyone knows, but that it is a necessary condition for survival is sometimes forgotten.

People also need the regard of their fellow human beings. They see themselves 'through the eyes of others' – as they think they are seen. In this way they form a *self-image*, which is determined by what they think other people think of them. They do not worry about everyone's opinion, but single out people from their past and present surroundings who are important to them. Thus people are also dependent on others for something as personal as their self-image or identity.

When people do something that they believe will attract the censure of others, they feel a sense of shame. They wish 'the earth would swallow them up' so that they did not have to 'face' their fellow human beings. People who feel that they have sunk very deep in the regard of others, and no longer command any respect, become extremely depressed and may even commit suicide. This also happens when a loved one is lost. Affection and regard can thus both be a matter of life and death.

People do their best to win the affection of others, in all sorts of ways. They try to become rich and famous, to rise to a high position or to distinguish themselves in sports, science or the arts. They do so partly for the pleasure it gives them, but also because they need the regard and affection of others.

The people with whom an individual maintains bonds of affection seldom form a very extensive network. There are generally only a few 'significant others' – loved or respected persons in the immediate surroundings, and people from the past who still play an important part in the person's memory and imagination. The approval or rejection of people who are somewhat further removed is also significant, but this tends to be expressed more vaguely as what 'they all' think: the opinion of 'the whole class', 'the entire neighbourhood', 'the people at work', or even 'the public'. These phrases reflect someone's good name, reputation or popularity, to honour and disgrace, to pride and shame. All such feelings are bound up in a network of dependencies – they are, supremely, social emotions.

Knowledge

People can only survive in society if they acquire the necessary knowledge. As small children they learn to talk, discovering how to make themselves intelligible and to understand what others say to them. They learn this mother tongue long before they go to school – it seems to happen 'by itself'. Small children also learn all kinds of practical skills at home, from dressing themselves and eating at the table to playing marbles and riding a bicycle. All the knowledge a person acquires comes from other people, sometimes casually – by following someone's example – and sometimes deliberately, by listening to teachers and studying textbooks.

In most countries, the majority of children attend elementary school for several years. In a particular country they will all learn roughly the same things. This is why the citizens of a country have a great deal of knowledge in common. On the other hand, children attend different schools when they are older and focus on diverse areas of knowledge. In this way, enormous differences in knowledge arise between the people of a single country. In other words, there is a common fund of *basic knowledge*, after which education fans out into different courses of varying length.

This education largely determines people's later occupation or career and hence their income, where they will live, how they will spend their leisure time, what kind of tastes they will develop, and even the kinds of opinions they are likely to have.

Since almost everyone in our society learns to read and write, and at least finishes elementary school, people who lack this basic knowledge are at a grave disadvantage. In centuries past, it was of little consequence if a peasant or workman was unable to read, write or make calculations, as they scarcely needed such skills for their work. Nowadays, however, this has all changed: everyone is assumed to be able to read instructions, newspapers and letters. Someone who cannot do so is labelled 'illiterate'. Once most of the people in a society can read and write, these skills are taken so much for granted that it becomes a matter of urgent necessity for those left behind to catch up. In this way, *a possibility for many becomes a necessity for everyone.*

The social arrangements within which someone lives determine what is, and what is not, essential knowledge. Thus we do not have to be able to distinguish the poisonous fruits in the woods from the nutritious ones, but for wood-dwellers such knowledge is indispensable to their survival. We, on the other hand, must be able to pick out the right coins and notes to pay for the fruit we have selected at the green-grocer's. All such skills, again, are learnt from other people.

People living in modern societies, then, need to know different things to cope with their world than do the inhabitants of the rain forest. But we do not know *more* about our world than they know about theirs. They may well be able to distinguish fifteen different snake species, while we are often at a loss to explain why the lights go on when we flick a switch, or why the aeroplane in which we are travelling stays in the air. Nor does this ignorance matter very much, for in our society there are always people who have specialized in a particular subject. The electrician or aviation engineer could explain it all to us. The essential knowledge is spread out among countless specialists, a social *division of knowledge* that makes it possible for us to do and use a million things without knowing much about them.

Small children are dependent for everything – including the first knowledge they acquire – on their immediate surroundings. In the past, children learnt what they needed to know in a small circle, and learnt it from experience, whether it was hunting, working the land or labouring in the workshop.

To learn to read and write, however, children have to go to school. Everything else they learn there builds on this initial knowledge of writing. As more young people attend more years of schooling, that schooling becomes increasingly essential for others who want to be admitted into the network in which the transfer of knowledge takes place.

Direction

Children not only have a great deal to learn, but they also have a great deal to unlearn. At an early age they have to learn to control their bowel movements until the right time and the right place. They may not grab whatever they want, and they are expected to finish what is on their plate. They must not fall asleep at school; they must go to bed, and get up, at certain set times. Gradually, natural bodily functions such as defecating, eating and sleeping are converted into habits which are acceptable to the outside world. In due course, the child is able to repress its natural inclinations and to give in to them at the appropriate time, in the lavatory, at the table, or in bed. This all happens without very much thought – almost automatically. The initial, natural inclinations are converted into a – social – second nature.

We cannot simply take whatever we choose from a shop counter. Someone who is angry is not free to take a club and smash someone else on the head. The watchword in every case is self-control. People must learn to control themselves and to refrain from actions that other people – and they themselves – deem unacceptable. But that is not all. People also have to learn to drive themselves to perform actions that other people – and they themselves – consider necessary. When the alarm-clock goes off, they have to force themselves to get up. Pupils must overcome a disinclination to turn off the television and do their homework. This 'self-driving' force means impelling yourself to do something, and preferably to do it well. As in riding a bicycle or driving a car, it is not enough to learn how to apply the brakes; you must also know how to accelerate in good time, and how to manoeuvre skilfully. People need to know how to drive themselves. For this, too, they need others to urge them along and steer them in the right direction. Self-control is a form of self-coercion: it makes people refrain from certain actions and perform others; it helps them to choose the right moment and the right place, and to do things in the proper way. People learn to drive themselves through the coercion exerted on them by others, in the first place by their parents – this is *external coercion.* But the world around us also puts us under pressure to 'coerce' ourselves; this is what is meant by expressions such as 'they have to want it themselves' or 'it is their own responsibility'. People are under *external coercion to coerce themselves.* Ultimately, they learn to control their impulses most of the time, without others having to exert constant pressure on them. This is *self-coercion.*

Every society has these three forms of coercion, though to differing degrees. The balance between them may also vary according to the particular situation. In some homes, children are not allowed to go out in the evenings; they are not given a key, and the door is simply locked. In other homes the father or mother will remind them that they have a test the next day and should go to bed on time, and there are still other homes where children come home when they please. At work and in the street, too, we come across these three types of coercion, in varying combinations.

People evidently need to learn how to control themselves in order to survive in society; and for this they need other people – directly at first, and later mostly indirectly. And here too, the relationships of dependence are strongest in the small circle of the family. The network later expands to include the school and the workplace. And it expands still further: in the background, for everyone, there are always inspectors and police officers maintaining external coercion. But in everyday life, most people are capable of controlling their actions themselves.

3 Societies: conditions for existence

A social arrangement may continue to exist even when all the people who originally belonged to it have gone. Mercedes, Manchester United and the Kingdom of the Netherlands all exist today, although the people who belonged to them in their earliest days have all been succeeded by others. Whenever a place falls vacant, because someone leaves or dies, someone else steps in to fill the gap. The newcomer must adapt upon joining, since all the surrounding positions are still occupied by the same people as before, who generally want things to carry on as in the past. But the new arrivals are never completely identical to their predecessors, and their adjustment is never total. If only for this reason, social arrangements are bound to change in the course of time.

Sometimes a sudden change may occur, for instance when an entire group of members depart and new people take their place. The editorial boards of magazines fill up vacancies by *co-opting*: they choose their new members themselves. But sometimes the editorial board is taken over at a stroke by a new generation. Can we still speak, then, of the same magazine?

It may also happen that a social arrangement ceases to exist because some members leave, and no one comes to take their place. Many villages in France have gradually died out with the older generation of inhabitants, because the young have left, and no new families have settled there.

Small social arrangements function within more comprehensive ones, and these in turn operate within society as a whole. This embedding in more wide-ranging arrangements heightens the continuity of a social arrangement.

The survival of a society depends on a number of conditions. Although the conditions for existence of the individuals who together make up a society are intimately bound up with those of the society as a whole, they are not exactly the same. The society does not eat or wear a coat, but to fulfil the human needs of food and shelter, it is essential that the goods required should be produced and distributed in that society. So the first condition that must be fulfilled, for a society to survive, is the *production and distribution* of the goods its people need.

The second essential condition is that consecutive generations be absorbed into roughly the same networks, so that the society regenerates itself – *reproduction.* This means not only that children are conceived and born, but that they are brought up, educated and instructed, and prepared to take their place in the adult world.

Just as individual people need protection, the society as a

14

whole requires protection against hostile forces from outside, in other words against other societies: *external security*. But for a society to survive, there must also be protection for the individuals of that society against one another: *internal security*.

Just as essential is a certain bond of affection between the members of a society, a sense of 'us' or a certain mutual confidence and *solidarity*.

Finally, a society can only continue if its members have ways of thinking that enable them to find their way about their social and physical surroundings, and which they can pass on to one another: *orientation*.

The necessary conditions for the continued existence of societies are thus directly related to the conditions for survival of individual people, but the two sets of conditions are not exactly the same. For a society is not simply 'a huge number of people', nor is it a sort of 'giant human being'. A society is a *configuration* of people in certain *patterns of interdependence*. This society continues to exist even when some of its members die or leave. But a society cannot continue to exist if the patterns of interdependence disintegrate, or if new people are not constantly absorbed into it. That is the difference.

4 Conclusion

We have taken a bird's-eye view of the terrain. People, it is clear, are dependent upon one another. To survive, six basic conditions must be fulfilled, for all of which people are reliant on others: food, shelter, protection, affection, knowledge and self-control. Each of these conditions links up with certain types of dependence, whether in a small circle or a much larger one. Networks of dependence change when people grow up; furthermore, those in ancient societies were different from those of today, and those in geographically separate countries also differ widely.

The continued existence of a society is related to the

survival of the people who live in it, but is not identical to it: a society continues to exist when its members have gone, as long as new people, arrayed in roughly the same patterns of interdependence, come to take their place.

2

How People are Connected to One Another

The previous chapter showed that people are interconnected. The following pages will examine these connections more closely. People have dealings with each other, but they do not have dealings with everyone to the same extent, or in the same way.

1 Networks

The members of a particular class at school all know each other by name. They say hello when they meet, and they all speak to each of their classmates now and then. Some see a great deal of each other, comparing notes on homework and going out together. Others have little contact. A few 'gangs' spend a lot of time in each other's company. One or two pupils 'don't belong' and go their own way. In each group of friends, one figure will often be the most active, suggesting ideas and occasionally bossing the others around. A few will be mere hangers-on.

Like all social arrangements, a class is a network or mesh of connections. We can picture lines for the connections, and junctions or nodes for the people who are linked. In this example, all the pupils will occasionally associate with one another. So they can all be linked with grey lines. But friends, who have more regular contact, may be pictured as linked by bolder connecting lines.

Every group of friends has its pacesetters and its hangers-on. One leads, the others follow. So the linking lines are directional. Arrows can be drawn between friends to indicate who tends to take the initiative and who is more inclined to follow. Often a single leader will have two or three close friends who each have followers of their own. This too can be indicated using arrows.

A situation in which everyone associates with everyone else is a fully connected network. A class at school is a fully connected network, but the links are light grey, as many of the relationships are superficial. Each group of friends is also a fully connected network, but the lines are much bolder, as the interaction is more intense.

Dutch schools draw up tree diagrams of each class, so that if the first lesson of the day is cancelled the message can be passed on efficiently: the first pupil to be told phones two others, who each call two classmates, and so on until the whole class has been informed. (It is evidently assumed that everyone has a telephone: a device that was once an option for many has long been a necessity for all – the same is now happening with the Internet.) In this message network, pupils are linked indirectly rather than directly, as each one has contact only with the single classmate who transmits the message and the next two on the list (until the last two, who have no one left to call).

A network of this kind is called a *hierarchical* or *tree network*. It consists of the smallest number of connections (*n* minus 1) that suffices to connect all (*n*) nodes, not directly, but through intermediaries. With its minimal number of links, this type of network is ideal for passing on messages. Here it can be done with the smallest possible number of telephone calls. That is why so many organizations are set up as hierarchical networks. One example is the army. A general issues his orders to a few colonels, who pass them on to the captains, their immediate subordinates; then the orders are relayed down the ranks until they reach the soldiers on the front line.

These network schemes can be used to illustrate all sorts of connections within a social arrangement. One example is a food supply network. A farming society, in which a large family provides for its own needs, is a small, close-knit network, and has relatively few connections with the outside world. The links are quite different in a money economy, where the farmers' food goes first to wholesalers and then to retailers before being purchased by other families. Even the obligations for neighbours to provide mutual assistance can be depicted in a network scheme, as can the relations between groups of warriors: you can draw lines to show who is fighting or threatening whom, and which groups have concluded alliances.

You could also draw an affective network of a class at secondary school, indicating who is in love with whom. A family tree is nothing more than a network of family relationships showing who married whom, and who is whose son or daughter. (A family tree is a tree network, but that is only because all sorts of branches are left out, in order to include either all the ancestors of one descendant or all the descendants of one ancestor.)

Sometimes the members of a network have no idea who they are linked to. In modern societies it is quite common not to know who your second cousins, great-uncles or great-aunts are, but members of traditional societies may well be able to name their third cousins twice removed. In modern societies, consumers can name the shop where they purchased something, but as for the rest of the network – wholesaler, manufacturer, supplier of raw materials – they are completely in the dark. Epidemiologists can try to reconstruct 'infection networks' tracing who has caught a disease from whom.

It is people who are the junctions of all these networks. Some occupy *central positions* – they are the nodes where numerous links converge. During a class at school, the teacher talks to the pupils, and they talk to the teacher. The pupils do not talk to each other (at least, that is not the idea). All communication proceeds through the teacher, who therefore occupies the central position in the network. Such central positions are generally linked to leadership, but this is not always the case. A company's telephone operator puts through all the calls, but there is no position of leadership associated with this central position, as a telephone operator is not supposed to take any part in the conversations or listen in.

In a hierarchical network, there are no direct links between lower-ranking members; they can only reach each other through someone higher up, more centrally placed in the network. Those occupying such central positions are better informed, can reach others more quickly and are themselves indispensable junctions for a larger number of people who may want to contact each other. This gives them a distinct advantage.

2   Networks and the course of life

The networks someone belongs to change as the years go by. Very small children are completely connected to their mother, who gives them food, shelter, love and protection. The mother herself is linked to others. The bond between mother and child is so strong that the two are sometimes referred to as a complex entity, the 'mother–child dyad'.

Infants soon develop relationships with other people they have contact with: their father, brothers and sisters, grandmother, grandfather and so on. Babies start to recognize the different people they meet and to distinguish between them. Children aged twelve months already play with friends, may attend a day nursery and get to know regular visitors and babysitters. A very small child is far more dependent on the people around it than they are on the child.

Once the child starts school, its network expands to include playmates and teachers. Older children go shopping, join sports clubs or take music lessons, go to the dentist, have different friends in the neighbourhood, and so on. Then comes secondary school, and new friendships replace older ones. When young people start work they make new relationships, with colleagues and the boss. Now many others depend upon them; customers and colleagues rely on the young recruits' achievements. Those who rise to management positions occupy a central place within the network, and others are particularly dependent on them. People marry and children are born, who are in turn dependent on the young parents. It is when men and women are in their 'prime' that others are most dependent on them.

The parents age, and their children leave home. At a certain age they stop work and start drawing their pensions. Later still, many friends and acquaintances are lost. The network shrinks again as fewer people are dependent on them, and they themselves gradually become dependent on a few carers when they are old and infirm. Thus the *balance of dependence* shifts in the course of a lifetime from maximum dependency on one caring figure to diverse mutual relationships of dependence with an increasing number of people, and finally to an increasingly one-sided dependence on a shrinking circle of people.

3 Kinship relations

Almost everyone belongs to kinship networks, such as families or clans. In traditional societies these kinship ties are by far the most important connections. Most relationships of dependence are embedded in family ties. This is why people who live in these societies are very well versed in matters of ancestors and kinsfolk. In societies of this kind, birth and descent come first, and an individual's own merits count for much less. There, you do not *achieve* a position through your own efforts, it is *ascribed* to you on the basis of parentage. Children – generally boys – inherit their father's land, and sons adopt their father's trade. Positions are also assigned on the basis of gender. Someone who is born a woman cannot attain the positions that are assigned to boys. Nor can men perform women's tasks. Positions such as tribal or village chief, lord of the manor and king are likewise assigned on the basis of descent. All this is taken for granted. Kingship falls to someone by birth, but in contemporary society this is highly exceptional, a practice anchored in tradition. Nowadays, although your background counts for a great deal – it helps to determine what kind of school you go to, and is very important when it comes to making useful connections – it does not dictate the rest of your life. Even the children of highly educated and wealthy parents are required to take examinations, apply for jobs and exert themselves to be promoted. If someone is given preferential treatment in a modern society on the basis of parentage or gender, it will rarely be done openly. On record, all that counts is what a person achieves; people have to attain their positions on their own merits.

Family relationships have retained their importance, but ties with distant relatives are not maintained so meticulously. People tend to live in nuclear families, separated from the outside world by the walls of their own home, which is often in a different town from their parents, brothers and sisters. But where it comes to affective ties, close relatives prove to have a strong sense of belonging, and in hardship they turn to each other for support.

4 Achieved relations

Most of our time is spent not with our families, but at school or at work, among people we have met and with whom we will eventually lose contact. This is characteristic of our society. Ties with classmates and teachers or colleagues, subordinates and superiors, are often fairly businesslike. They focus on the work that has to be done in the shared surroundings. This is why people spend a lot of time figuring out how to tackle this work together with (or sometimes in spite of) others around them. Within the network of school and work, 'informal' relations also evolve that may be quite emotional – pupils make friends and enemies. Members of a shared network also join other networks, such as sports clubs and churches. Each one brings them into contact with new acquaintances, who often do not visit or even know each other. So a member of modern society will often belong to several networks, doing different things, associating with different acquaintances, and even behaving differently in each one. Someone may have many faces. 'He never says a word at school, but at the football club he always hogs the conversation', or 'If my mother were to see me now . . .'. As time passes a person will join new networks and leave others. Such changes of network – and in someone's position within a network – go together with changes of attitude and conduct.

In modern societies we have *friendship networks* alongside those based on kinship. People who attended the same school, lived on the same street, belonged to the same student club or performed military service together may remain friends throughout their lives, enjoying each other's company and drawing on their acquaintance in their quest for a suitable job, a good house or a partner. A network of this kind is particularly useful for making new contacts when members do not all know each other (in other words, the network is not fully connected) but when certain members have an extensive web of contacts outside the network. This leads to inquiries such as, 'Hey, do you know a good dentist?' or 'Any idea who may have a room to rent?' Mediators between two networks that are only weakly connected are often indispensable links in the chain of information. We may speak, paradoxically, of 'the strength of weak links'.

5   Indirect ties

The world is sometimes smaller than you think. You may well have had the experience of meeting a stranger in a foreign country and discovering in the course of the conversation that you share a common acquaintance. What a coincidence! How is it possible?

Every adult knows about 1,000 people by name and face. So the thousand people I know must each know another thousand. Leaving the overlaps out of consideration, my acquaintances would know a total of one million people. If I meet a stranger in new surroundings, it is not unlikely that this will be one of the million people who know one of my thousand acquaintances. This likelihood is increased by the fact that when people travel, although they move through space, they remain in the same social sphere. In other words, they choose a resort frequented by their fellow townspeople or others of the same religious faith, by people with roughly the same sort of work or of the same age: 'Birds of a feather flock together.' This obviously boosts the probability of two people who meet turning out to have a common acquaintance. Businesspeople and university lecturers travel a great deal, but as they remain within their network of business relations or fellow academics, they tend to meet mainly people 'of their own kind'.

Indirect networks are very useful for making connections. For instance, a politician will set out to build up good relations with many different acquaintances who each have a great many connections and can hence act as mediators with the electorate. In this way, contact can be maintained – indirectly – with many hundreds of thousands of voters.

6   The unfolding of networks

In the past, most members of the society would live their lives within a fairly small, closed, fully and multiply connected network. They lived within a circle of relatives and neighbours, in which everyone knew one another ('completely connected'), and most had little contact with the outside world. They had a great deal to do with one another in many different ways ('multiply connected'). The woman next door, for instance, was a cousin by marriage, and assisted at the birth of children in the village. When a goat was slaughtered, she would receive a share, and she would keep the village church clean. The village head was also the baker, besides which he would help to resolve quarrels and he would lend someone a sack of flour if need be, as was only right considering he was the eldest son of the richest family in the village.

In the development towards modern societies we see networks *unfolding*. The small, closed, fully and multiply connected networks of the past are expanding; they become less closed as some of their members make contact with the outside world. If the baker's brick oven breaks down, he goes off to town to buy a new steel oven – and to do so, he will have to take out a loan from the bank. The daughter of the woman who assisted at births will enrol as a college student to train as a midwife, and when she returns she may well have a fiancé with her, a man from outside the village.

As this trend progresses, relations become less multiple and more specific. A new salaried post of mayor is created, and the baker no longer intervenes in village disputes. Those who find they have too little flour for their needs go to the town hall and apply for welfare. Experienced neighbours or aunts are no longer called in to assist when a baby is due, as the village now has its own qualified midwife to do the job. When a goat is slaughtered, the meat that cannot be eaten immediately is not sent to the neighbours, but stored in the freezer. And so on. Another gradual development is that the network is no longer fully linked up. The villagers do not have so much to do with one another any more, and time goes by without them even meeting. Newcomers settle in the village, and not everyone knows who they are.

This process leads to an unfolding of what was originally

a small, closed, fully and multiply connected network. The villagers have more contact with the outside world, and within the network some links are severed or lose their multiple functions. This process of the unfolding of networks is characteristic of the transition from traditional to modern societies, in which village communities are absorbed into a money economy with industrial production, large organizations and state intervention.

3

What People Expect of One Another

People make up networks of dependencies, but also of *expectations*. And just as all individuals are nodes, or junctions, in networks of dependencies, they are also nodes in networks of expectations vested in them. Most of these expectations turn out right most of the time. They scarcely impinge upon our consciousness; they speak for themselves, or rather, they do not 'speak' at all. It is only when an expectation fails to materialize that we are jolted into an awareness of what we have always taken for granted.

1 Roles

Everyone assumes that motorists will drive on the correct side of the road. They scarcely think about it. They coolly hurtle towards each other at 70 miles an hour, each blithely confident that the oncoming car will keep to the rules. And it almost always does. But occasionally someone will be spotted driving against the traffic, and panic breaks out. Radio programmes are interrupted to warn listeners of the 'ghost driver'. In this case the expectations are based on rules, on the highway code. It is assumed that the rules will be respected, partly because anyone who does drive on the wrong side of the motorway is risking his own life as well as those of others. In principle we take it for granted that others are in possession of their faculties, that they will act reasonably: that they would do nothing to cause unnecessary harm to themselves or others.

Some expectations have little to do with laws, nor with reasonableness, but are based on *customs or conventions*. 'That is simply how we do things around here.' There is no law stating that people should extend their right hand, and not their left, on meeting. Shaking left hands would in principle be just as reasonable and convenient. But in our society it would clash with the accepted norms and therefore baffle people's expectations. It would not be unlawful or unreasonable, simply discourteous.

Let us now move away from general expectations, which apply to most people, and look at those which are more specific, having to do with the position someone occupies in a network. A waitress is expected to bring customers their orders. If a customer got up and fetched a piece of apple pie from the kitchen instead of waiting to be served it would certainly raise some eyebrows. The waitress expects customers to place orders, to pay before leaving, and so forth. You could easily write a book about how customers expect waitresses to behave and vice versa. Some of these expectations are not entirely clear: you may well feel unsure when it comes to tips, and it feels uncomfortable not to know exactly what is expected of you.

The set of expectations of someone who occupies a particular position in a given society is referred to as that person's *role*. This term comes from the vocabulary of the stage, where it relates to the part an actor learns – the words the rest of the cast expect to hear. In everyday life we have the mother's role, the leader's role, the waitress's role and so forth. Someone playing a particular role knows what expectations are aroused (what the role entails), as do those encountering the person playing that role (they know what may be expected of such a person). We may therefore speak of *shared expectations*.

Someone who is able to operate within society shares the whole spectrum of general expectations (those based on the law, reasonableness and convention) and is familiar with those attached to specific roles. Just by growing up in society one becomes a competent member of that society, familiar with volumes of unwritten knowledge. But in this respect, interaction is much like walking: you can be perfectly competent without making any conscious effort. Parties are governed by such unwritten rules. Upon arrival you greet those already present in different ways: you may shake hands with the first, kiss the second, embrace the third and slap the fourth on the back. You do all of this without stopping to think what the rules are. People negotiate society without needing to consult a manual.

Expectations in regard to someone in a particular position do not always coincide. Should a shopkeeper always be prepared to change a large note, or to give a customer small change for a parking meter? Some customers expect it, while other customers – and many shopkeepers – take a different point of view.

Even when all those concerned have identical expectations of a particular role, there may still be *incompatible expectations.* Hospital patients all expect nurses to wash them, change their sheets and dressings and administer their medication in the correct manner and at the correct time. And nurses expect no less of themselves. But patients and nursing staff alike also expect nurses to be ready to express interest and words of comfort every minute of the day. There is often too little time. As a result, nurses fail to meet the expectations that go with their role, including those they have of themselves. This produces a *role conflict*: incompatible expectations in relation to a specific role.

The fabric of expectations makes social life predictable: usually everything goes according to our expectations. This simplifies the business of society enormously. There is no need to wind down your car window and shout and gesture to the driver of each oncoming car to indicate which direction you intend to go: you simply keep straight on. At the baker's there is no need to ask another customer how one acquires a loaf of bread, who is allowed to take one or whether payment is required. When you reach the front of the queue (taking care to mind your turn) you tell someone behind the counter what you want, you are told how much it costs, you pay and the loaf is yours. The unquestioning confidence that our unthought expectations will be borne out simplifies the business of society, and creates order in it, usually.

2   The Thomas rule

People let themselves be guided by their expectations. When school breaks up for the summer holidays, shopkeepers without school-age children may nonetheless close the shop for a time in this period, because they expect business to be sluggish. Wholesalers too anticipate a lull in trade, and plan their own holiday at the same time. Banks and transport firms that trade with the wholesalers and retailers assume that everything will grind to a halt in August and send their staff on holiday as well. In short, business is expected to be slow in this period, and as a result it is slower still. Meanwhile, at the holiday resorts, expectations of large summer crowds make it even busier: there, of course, the shops will stay open and actually take on extra staff, and all sorts of festivities and recreational activities are organized, attracting even more holiday-makers. At the same time there are counter-movements: people without school-age children go on holiday at other times of the year, work permitting, precisely to avoid the crowds.

This is summarized by the Thomas rule: *when people expect something to happen, these expectations affect what happens.* This can work in many different ways, including *self-confirming expectations* and *self-refuting expectations.*

The example of the quiet holiday period is a case of expectations confirming themselves. Here is another example. A rumour starts to spread that butter and soap may well become scarce. This arouses the expectation that butter and soap may be unobtainable in the near future, triggering a run on the shops and an outbreak of stockpiling.

A few panic-buying days later, the shelves have been emptied of butter and soap. The rumour has aroused expectations that have been borne out precisely because people acted on the basis of those expectations.

Sometimes the reverse occurs – expectations can prove 'self-refuting'. A television documentary shows a lovely, unspoilt village where prices are still as low as 20 years ago, and where seaside visitors can spend their summers in peace and quiet. The documentary itself puts an abrupt end to all that. In the expectation of finding a tranquil holiday spot at a reasonable price, visitors descend on the featured village in their thousands and the few available rooms are suddenly let out at outrageous prices. The documentary aroused expectations that failed to be fulfilled precisely because many people acted on the basis of these expectations.

3 Disrupted expectations

Sometimes events shatter patterns of expectation. If a country is occupied by a hostile foreign power, for instance, people may be uncertain of what to expect from one another, unsure of who can be relied upon. It is no longer clear what the rules are – what the occupying force forbids and what it will allow. You wonder whether your neighbour will give you away if you defy a ban on listening to the radio, and whether old acquaintances will share their supplies with you. Will you get into trouble with your boss if you give your opinion of the occupying force at your place of work? Do you really have to say 'Comrade' instead of 'Sir' at work these days? Not only are new laws passed by the occupying force, all sorts of customs suddenly cease to apply, the *conventions* are suspended and society as a whole is dislocated.

A dislocation of this kind can also occur in peacetime. The sudden closure of a company can overturn expectations of life among the entire workforce. People who had counted on keeping their jobs until retirement are suddenly unemployed, compelled to sell their houses and seek work elsewhere, to put their children in different schools, sell the car and so forth. Even those who succeed in finding new jobs may well have to accept a lower salary, and the less fortunate have no alternative but to apply for benefit. Under the new circumstances their families must adapt to one another again, and tensions mount within the home. The neighbourhood is put out of joint as a result: shops go bankrupt because the company's ex-employees are short of money or leave, schools may have to close for lack of pupils. All this is accompanied by enormous confusion, insecurity and fear.

On a smaller scale, expectations may collapse within a single family, on a street or among a group of fellow workers, in the wake of an extra-marital affair or a case of robbery or fraud. People no longer know what to expect from each other, their confidence has been undermined, and the business of society – of living life together – suddenly becomes unpredictable and laborious. Society is a fabric of expectations, and within that fabric there may be weaving faults and gaping tears.

4 Blind process

People have expectations of one another, act on the basis of these expectations, and all these actions affect each other, often in unexpected ways. Whatever we set out to achieve, we are dependent on others at every turn and in every possible way: we are part of networks made up of chains of dependence. Our actions have consequences for others, just as we are affected by what others do. But it is not always possible to take in the whole picture, to see beforehand how these chains of dependence work. Because of this, the consequences of our actions are often quite different from what was intended. Such unintentional consequences are a result of the interplay between the actions of people who, while dependent upon one another, are unable to grasp all the patterns of dependence involved.

Hence developments within a society are predominantly the result of human expectations, but the end result is often something no one had expected or intended: it is the outcome of a *blind process.* Many people want to be able to live in the major cities, to be close to their jobs. Because so many people settle there, diverse new companies are attracted to the city because of the large potential workforce it has to offer. But as time passes, so many factories and offices congregate in the city that the land becomes too expensive to build private houses there. Residential neighbourhoods start being built on the outskirts of the city instead. Those who move into them have to commute to their jobs in the city centre, enduring hours of traffic congestion or overcrowded trains and buses to and from their work every day. No one had intended or foreseen this, and yet it is the composite result of the expectations and actions of a great many separate individuals. It is the outcome of a blind process.

4

How People Distinguish Themselves from One Another: Stratifications

People differ in all sorts of ways: there are differences between adults and children, men and women, established groups and newcomers, employers and employees, the highly educated and the uneducated, light-skinned and dark-skinned people, people of different religions and so forth. Some differences stem from characteristics already fixed at conception, while others develop in the course of life. But all perceptible differences between people are *socially formed*: that is to say, within each society a certain significance and certain expectations will be attached to them, and these will help determine their impact. The Thomas rule introduced in the previous chapter applies here too: if something is expected to happen, these expectations affect what actually happens.

Certain differences between men and women stem from the moment of conception: several sex-specific genes lead to divergent paths of development, both before and after birth. These genetically derived disparities are called *sexual differences*. But sexual differences in turn lead to countless social distinctions, socially formed in ways known as *gender differences*, which differ from one society to the next. Though sexual differences are the same everywhere, in some societies they lead to enormous gender differences: women must be

34

covered from head to toe and stay at home most of the time, while in others men and women wear similar clothes, and women can do most of the jobs men do outside the home. Some differences between people greatly affect social interaction. The larger they are, the more *unequal social relations* prevail. These are of three kinds: power relations, property relations and prestige relations. The three types of social inequality occur in almost every society, but to a very different degree. And they also determine relationships between men and women, young and old, established groups and newcomers, and often between people of lighter or darker skin colour.

1 Power relations

Power relations are dependence relations with a minus sign. If A is dependent on B to achieve something, this creates a relationship of dependence between them. At the same time, there is a power relationship between them. B has power over A – the power to help fulfil A's needs or not. People are always embedded in power and dependence relations with others.

When someone says, 'X has power', what is really meant is 'X has power over A, B and C', which implies that A, B, and C are more dependent on X than vice versa. Within the network of power and dependence relations that X, A, B and C constitute, X is in a *position of power*. The more people there are in a network of power and dependence relationships who depend more on someone than that person does on them, the stronger is that central individual's position of power within the network.

There is always a certain *balance of power*: within a network, certain individuals are dependent on someone, who is in turn dependent on them (and on others). If others depend more heavily on one individual than vice versa, the person in question has a *positive* balance. This is only a manner of speaking, however, as it is almost impossible to measure and compare relationships of power and dependence to determine where the balance lies.

At school, pupils are dependent on their teachers in all sorts of ways; they need the material to be explained and their assignments to be marked. Teachers are not so dependent on each individual pupil. In other words, teachers are in a position of power *vis-à-vis* their pupils within the network of relationships in a classroom. Still, it only takes a few pupils to ruin the atmosphere or disrupt a class, so that to keep order the teacher is dependent on the pupils as a group. If no pupils at all turn up for class, the teacher will be out of a job. Nor can teachers act arbitrarily or do as they please; they have to follow a curriculum and they are under an obligation to explain the material and to adhere to certain standards when assessing pupils' work. Within the framework of these rules, teachers have certain discretionary powers. But they in turn are dependent on the school management, parents and the education inspectorate.

Hence power is a characteristic of a position within a network of power and dependence relations. People who occupy *positions of power* are 'in power' for as long as they stay there. Yet to stay there, they are dependent on all those who are dependent on them. And outside the network, those positions of power do not count for very much.

So who actually has 'the' power? This is an interesting question, but one that must usually remain unanswered. There is a distribution of power within a network; in other words, the network may be characterized by more or less asymmetrical power relations. Hence within a network of power and dependence relations some have relative positions of power (a positive balance) and others have positions largely characterized by dependence (a negative balance). But how does this distribution of power come about, and how does it change? In other words, how does the process of *power formation* work?

Power relations form in the course of time, and follow from previous power and dependence relations. In human society the slate is never wiped clean: something has always gone before, and lives on in people's memories. Expectations are formed on the basis of those memories, affecting what comes later. The pattern of dependence between teacher and pupils is anchored in the network of the school, which may have existed for many decades, and is linked to a tradition of education going back several centuries. It is this previous history that has shaped today's relations between teachers and pupils.

A position of power is always linked to the dependencies of others. Hence someone who can fulfil the needs of others is in a relative position of power. A mother is in a position of near-absolute power over her small children, as they depend upon her for all their needs. Physically strong individuals can create dependence by issuing threats or by offering protection from outside attack. Someone who is armed is in an even stronger position of power in relation to those who are unarmed. But in a regulated society, power based on the exercise of violence is restrained by legislation and the maintenance of law and order.

Affection can be a vehicle of power: people are willing to put up with a great deal for fear of losing the affection or respect of important people in their surroundings. Within the family, parents' power over their children may sometimes be based on the implicit warning, 'If you do that, I won't love you any more'. Children too can impose their will and exert power by manipulating their parents' feelings. Even infants possess a certain power, as their crying will generally get them what they want.

Purveyors of specialized knowledge also acquire a position of power in relation to those who believe they need such knowledge: sorcerers, priests, doctors, lawyers, and even teachers possess exclusive knowledge of this kind, and as the saying goes: knowledge is power.

People are also dependent on others to direct their own actions, and this in turn can be a means for others to exercise power over them. We constantly take our cue from signals transmitted by others around us. Sometimes these signals may be blatant and unambiguous, whereas at other times –

perhaps when dealing with dress codes at work, for instance – they may be subtle and implicit. Once we reach adulthood we are generally more capable of steering our own actions and less in need of others to coerce us to coerce ourselves. We set the alarm clock ourselves, and actually get up when it goes off. In that sense we become 'more independent', more autonomous, less reliant on the constant inspection and correction of others. Yet even after reaching maturity, we have our own private radar devices that scan the surroundings for any response to our behaviour, and often derive strength from the gentle insistence of others to enhance our self-control. For instance, alcoholics trying to shake off their addiction may well join Alcoholics Anonymous; without the support and social pressure of their peers they are unable to resist the temptation to drink.

Any way in which people are dependent on others is potentially a way in which others can exert power over them. All exercise of power takes place within a network. Certain positions in a network are more suitable for the formation of power than others. The centre is associated with power. It is easier for someone to influence the expectations of others from the centre than from the periphery, which means it is also easier to steer their behaviour. This is the role of the team manager in a cycling race, who has a good view of the whole field from his following car. Someone in this position acts as *coordinator*. From the centre, you can also exploit relations with one person to fulfil the needs of another: this is the role of an *agent*, such as a marriage broker who knows all the marriageable boys and girls for miles around.

Another way of acquiring a position of power is by *manipulation* – by tampering with the expectations of people who, while not directly linked to one another, are all directly linked to the manipulator. A hostess who wants to bring together a great many important and interesting people at her dinner party will first approach a prominent figure and mention that another leading light is sure to attend: then the first VIP will be willing to come. This prepares the ground for the next phone call, and so on. Has the hostess lied? Certainly, but it was a self-confirming lie, a lie that converts itself into truth because of the expectations it arouses.

From a central position you can also play people off against one another: a clever politician can persuade one party's supporters that they will never get their way, because the other party's supporters will oppose them. The same argument can then be used with the other party, and eventually the manipulator at the heart of the web will be able to drive through a compromise proposal without too much opposition from either side. The manipulator can even decide to fuel the enmity between the two parties, so as to prevent them from dealing directly with one another and to remain indispensable to the parties' efforts to find a solution: this is the *divide and rule* strategy.

The *kingship mechanism* was based on much the same principle: kings would consolidate their position of power in the kingdom *vis-à-vis* other noble houses by turning them against one another. At a later stage, the kings could further strengthen their power base by sometimes supporting the nobility against the bourgeoisie, and at other times supporting the bourgeoisie against the nobility. In modern societies, governments often control their armed forces by separating them: army, navy and air force compete for funding from the budget, which stops them forming a united front against the government.

In all these examples, the person occupying a position of power has a direct link to the others in the network, who are not linked directly to each other: this corresponds to the pattern of a hierarchical network. People in a position of power can take advantage of this position to strengthen it; alternatively, they may bungle and forfeit it. In this sense, the formation of power also depends on the individual or the group that occupies a relative position of power.

In some modern societies politicians are elected by all adult citizens, and they are therefore dependent on the voters. In a *democracy* of this kind, voters have a measure of power over the political leaders who in turn exercise

democracy
= less unequal
power relations

power over the population. [The power relations are less unequal than in societies in which the population does not elect its leaders.]

The networks in which power is formed may be very large and complex. This can make it hard to see where the balance of power lies, where the centres of power are situated, and which groups one is most dependent on. This is especially true of relationships of economic power, which sometimes span oceans and embrace millions of people in networks of production and trade. An employee in one country may become redundant because of price movements on the other side of the world; the price paid to growers for their coffee beans may suddenly rise because in some remote country import duties on coffee have been slashed.

When relationships of power are generally accepted, they may be called *relationships of authority*. What this means is that people assume that good reasons could be given for the exercise of power – reasons with which they would agree. It is not even necessary for this justification to be provided in so many words, as long as the population is confident that *legitimation* is feasible – that good arguments exist. It takes far fewer power resources to implement measures with authority than with threats and coercion.

2 Property relations

Property entails the actual power to dispose of goods, including land and livestock. So at first sight it appears to be a kind of relationship of power over things, but in fact it relates to people – namely, to those who do not have those goods at their disposal. Hence property means both having goods at one's disposal and excluding others from disposing of them: it is an *exclusive power of disposal*. People can use their property to make others dependent on them. Thus property is also a power resource and a property relationship is a special type of power relationship.

In *nomadic societies* – comprising itinerant hunter-gatherers who feed off the animals and plants they encounter on their travels – no crops are sown, and the land is not cultivated. Durable tools are virtually non-existent, dwellings are abandoned as the company moves on, little if anything is preserved, so that there is scarcely any question of property. In fact, many nomadic peoples shun all forms of storage, discarding their utensils after a while, possibly to prevent the envy and competition that such property could arouse.

Property can only be acquired when people bring forth something durable: when they cultivate the land, produce durable goods and store supplies. This happens when they settle somewhere for a relatively long period and adapt the natural surroundings to their needs: by clearing the land of stones and undergrowth, making it even, sowing food crops and eliminating all competing plant life ('weeds'), fertilizing and irrigating the land (or reclaiming it from the sea, as in the Netherlands). This is the phase of *agricultural revolution*: when people no longer move from place to place in search of food, but turn one place into a suitable food-supplying environment. Having taken this step, they want their efforts to be rewarded and to keep the harvest for themselves. They build up stocks to guard against famine, store seeds for the next season and use durable tools such as ploughs and storage pots, build dwellings and sheds, rear draught animals and livestock for slaughter, dairy cattle and so forth. This can provoke envy and covetousness on the part of those who have no land, no supplies or durable goods: 'Thou shalt not covet thy neighbour's house, thou shalt not covet thy neighbour's wife, nor his manservant, nor his maidservant, nor his ox, nor his ass, nor any thing that is thy neighbour's' (Exodus 20: 17).

Because property implies by definition the exclusion of others, property relations can only endure when this exclusion can be effectively maintained. Property also calls for a non-aggression pact with other possessors, and means that possessors must defend their goods from the *propertyless* – in *agricultural societies* this means the landless, and in *industrial societies* it means those who do not possess land, factories or machinery, or financial assets.

Property relations result from conquest, gifts, inheritance, exchange or purchase: they are justified by rules of law. Ownership is the lawful possession of property. Someone who possesses property is the only one who can dispose of it, whereas someone who owns it is the only one who is *entitled* by law to dispose of it. Property relations are based on the power of disposal and ultimately on relationships of power, whereas ownership relations are also based on rules of law.

Property relations in turn have repercussions on relationships of power. Property that can be used in production is known collectively as *capital*. In agricultural societies the possession of land is the most important asset. The land often yields more than the farmers themselves need to survive: this food surplus can serve as subsistence for those who do not work the land themselves, such as priests and warriors. Someone with a great deal of land can maintain an army from the food surplus; conversely, someone with an army can seize land and defend it from others.

With the rise of industrial societies, the possession of *means of production* other than land became important: machines, vehicles and factory buildings made up the industrial capital. Industry also produces all kinds of consumer goods that do not serve as a means of production, but that directly provide for consumers' needs, such as cars, refrigerators and televisions. Most people's property consists of such durable consumer goods, including their own home.

In *post-industrial society*, knowledge has become even more important, especially in the production process, so much so that people's knowledge and skills are now also regarded as a means of production, their *cultural capital*, property that can be acquired through education.

Unlike power, property can be measured, in terms of money. The value of someone's property expressed in money is that person's *capital*. Capital is distributed very unevenly among the population: the richest 5% of the Dutch population owns approximately half the total private capital in the Netherlands. Even so, the distribution of wealth has become more balanced over the past hundred years: in 1894 the wealthiest 5% owned about 80% of the total. An increasingly large proportion of capital has come into the hands of funds that receive contributions from working people and pay benefit to those who are unable to work because of illness, disability, redundancy or old age. In times of need they can hence rely on the collective capital amassed in these funds, but their own, private capital, of which they may freely dispose, is generally small.

3 Prestige relations

The arrival of a particular person may cause all those present to rise to their feet, nod, applaud or even bow: shortly afterwards, someone else comes in, and everyone carries on talking without even acknowledging the newcomer's presence. The first visitor was apparently a very important one, whereas the second has less standing in this company.

Group photographs often make it very clear who are important: they stand at the front, in the middle, or higher than the others. In old paintings, the people of most consequence were depicted larger than the rest. Important people are described as 'prominent', 'at the centre', 'highly placed' or 'grand'. They are looked up to and people listen to what they have to say.

Evidently there is a ranking order among people, depending on the position they occupy within a particular network. The higher their rank, the greater their prestige. Prestige is the value that others attach to an individual occupying a particular network position. Prestige exists only in the eyes of others: it is quite literally the 'regard' in which someone is held.

People may derive prestige from anything in which they are better or higher or more than others, as long as it counts in the estimation of those around them. In the United States, people whose ancestors came to that country long ago are held in higher regard than those from families who have not lived there for very long. (Yet the descendants of the people who have lived there longest, Native Americans, are held in low esteem by other Americans.) In Europe, people who can trace their family tree back to the Middle Ages derive prestige from this (and yet everyone has ancestors from that time and indeed from the hundreds of thousands of years before; where would they have suddenly come from otherwise?).

Prestige is made visible and consolidated by all sorts of insignia: medals for courage, awards for merit, and sports trophies. The Netherlands accords more importance than the United States to titles and other forms of address such as 'the Honourable', 'Professor' and 'Doctor' – all of them visible signs of prestige.

People may also vaunt and increase their prestige by displaying their possessions, by the clothes they wear and the cars they drive. The prestige of the leading lights in society is also confirmed by the places they occupy: grandstand spectator seats, a box at the theatre, first-class compartments in trains and aeroplanes, the VIP lounge, a luxury suite in a five-star hotel, and so on. A house with extensive grounds and a drive, and with numerous large rooms, will enhance the status of those who live there. Preferential treatment and the possession of luxury items are of course in themselves sources of pleasure and comfort, but they also emit signals to others that they are dealing with persons of consequence.

In present-day society, the mere fact of putting in frequent appearances on television is sufficient to confer prestige. Such individuals are held in high regard, even if all they do is present the weather report or hand out prizes to quiz contestants.

Prestige may also be based on special courage or endurance, for instance in the case of Resistance heroes, or on great wisdom or on an unusual willingness to make sacrifices. But however great these virtues may be, someone's prestige arises from the regard in which the person is held by others, the place accorded to that person in a ranking order of importance. And all prestige is based on comparisons: for every higher there must be a lower, for every greater there must be a lesser. Regard for one means disdain for another. Prestige relations are by their nature unequal. For people within a social arrangement it is almost impossible to avoid such comparisons; at best they can try to impose their own ranking order of prestige ('he may not be a great scholar, but he can run like the wind'). Sometimes a person's prestige applies only within a small circle: jazz musicians are held in high regard by jazz enthusiasts, whereas popular musicians are appreciated far more widely.

In contemporary societies, prestige derives more from individual achievement than from inherited positions, it is more often acquired than bestowed, whereas in earlier societies status was primarily based on descent. Another characteristic of today's societies is the multiplicity of ranking orders that may apply simultaneously within different networks or even within a single network: for instance on the basis of wealth, fame, erudition, or achievements in art or sports.

There is a close connection between relations of power, property and prestige. Powerful people will generally also have more prestige, but not always. The two dimensions coincide, for instance, in cabinet ministers, who not only hold positions of power in the network known as government, but are also held in high regard. This is reflected in the special position they occupy at ceremonial occasions and the attention and precedence they are given by those around them. But one position may give more power, while another brings more prestige: an obscure government official may decide on a subsidy to be awarded to a greatly respected artist.

Property too often goes hand in hand with prestige, but not always, and not automatically. Property must be displayed if it is to confer status. A drug dealer, however wealthy, is held in less regard than the poorly paid investigator who catches him (although he may enjoy considerable prestige in certain underworld circles).

When a gap opens up between the position someone occupies in the ranking order of power or property and the same person's position in the ranking order of prestige, we speak of a *status discrepancy*. This applies not only to a person with a great deal of power or property and little status, but equally to someone with high status but little power or property. The *nouveaux riches*, war profiteers and 'yuppies' have plenty of property, little power and fairly low status – the very terms used to describe them reflect contempt. On the other hand, many spiritual leaders, artists and scholars have little property or power, but are held in high regard.

Status conversion is the term used to describe the conversion of power into property and prestige or vice versa. A cabinet minister may be offered a place on the board of directors of a multinational after resigning from government; that is a case of power being converted into property. A more pregnant example is a politician or senior public servant abusing that position to accept bribes – a form of conversion known as *corruption*. The opposite movement is exemplified by the landowner who hires soldiers and the entrepreneur who donates to an election fund. Then there is the conversion from power to prestige – the cabinet minister who has her official portrait made, or who is decorated with a medal of honour – in the United Kingdom, former ministers may be granted a peerage. Property can be converted into esteem, in the case of multi-millionaires who show off their wealth by extravagant displays of luxury, or who make large donations to charitable or cultural funds – when commercial businesses do this, it is called sponsorship. We see the conversion of prestige into power in the case of the film star who is elected president, and the conversion of prestige into property in the case of a member of a prominent family who secures a well-paid position in business or a wealthy spouse solely on the basis of birth.

4 Stratification

Each society has social layers, or strata, which are demarcated more or less sharply from one another, whereas within each social stratum, people occupy roughly similar positions. The formation of these social strata is called *stratification*. In a highly stratified society, the differences between people in different strata are pronounced, and embrace all three ranking orders simultaneously – that is, power, property and prestige.

Slave societies are the most highly stratified of all, with the upper layer having almost unlimited power over those at the bottom, whom they exclude from possessing property and deny any prestige. Slaves occupy a position approaching that of animals: they are the property of slave-holders. Slavery existed in antiquity, and until the mid-nineteenth century it was still a universal feature of plantations in the Western hemisphere, in the South of the United States and also, for instance, in the former European colonies of the Caribbean. The Africans who fell into the hands of the traffickers became slaves, and likewise all their descendants, unless they were among the fortunate few who escaped or were permitted to buy their freedom.

In a *caste society*, too, birth determines position, and the differences between castes are sharply defined. In India, where the caste system was universal, and where it still exists today in a somewhat diluted form, the ranking order was in the first place one of prestige: the priests' caste was held in highest esteem, followed by that of warriors and then that of farmers and artisans. At the bottom of the heap was – and is – the caste of the 'untouchables'. In principle it is impossible ever to change your caste, which is determined at birth. Members of lower castes could certainly amass property, and in today's India they can also rise to positions of power; nevertheless, members of lower castes are still predominantly poorer and less powerful than those higher up the caste system.

Stratifications

In pre-industrial Europe, society was also divided into fairly strict layers – it was a society of *estates*, in which the nobility and clergy each constituted an estate, while a third estate comprised farmers, merchants and craftsmen. Here too, birth was the decisive factor, and differences in power, property and prestige roughly paralleled the dividing lines between the estates. The children of farmers and craftsmen, like those of the nobility, could join the clergy, albeit only in the lower ranks. In large parts of Europe, including Poland and Russia, a system of serfdom persisted well into the nineteenth century: the bondmen of an overlord were not permitted to depart from the land without his permission, were required to perform forced labour, and had to surrender a proportion of their harvest by way of lease.

With the industrial revolution, new social strata came into existence. Aside from landowners, a group arose that could dispose of the new means of production, such as factories and machines: the bourgeoisie or propertied classes. Those without property worked in the factories and mines for wages: they constituted the *proletariat*, or *working classes*. In this *class society*, descent was still important, but the distinction between the classes was based on property relations, centring on the possession of the means of production. It was possible for a small entrepreneur to go bankrupt and be forced to work for wages, whereas some workers rose to become entrepreneurs, and in turn employed others to work their machines.

Alongside bourgeoisie and proletariat, there was still a middle class of *self-employed* people – farmers who worked their own land, craftsmen with their own workshops, employing at most a few assistants, and shopkeepers running their own businesses. In the past century and a half, a *new middle class* has arisen, of people who, while working for wages in large organizations (within government or commercial companies) are highly educated and occupy key management positions. These 'salaried classes' are an increasingly large intermediate group, which merge seamlessly into the working class at one end (at the level of clerical staff, for instance) and the bourgeoisie at the other end (for instance in the case of directors who do not own their companies). In this century many shopkeepers who have been unable to compete with chain stores have closed their businesses and taken management positions at supermarkets, thus moving from the petty bourgeoisie to the salaried middle classes.

In the course of their lives, people may move from one stratum to another: they may prove social climbers ('from newspaper boy to millionaire') or they may suffer social decline (from financial whizzkid to jailbird). Any movement of this kind, whether upward or downward, is a case of *social mobility*. This mobility may manifest itself within an individual's life, but it may also occur from one generation to the next. Often the son will achieve more than his father, and the granddaughter will go further still: the father was a peat worker, the son becomes a schoolteacher and the grand-daughter may make it to professor. In caste societies social mobility is rare, in class societies it occurs more often because of the greater emphasis on achievement than on family background: positions are more often attained than ascribed. Most parents cannot leave their children a large amount of capital, nor can they offer them prospects within a family business; what they can do, however, is provide them with a good education, which will become their cultural capital. Formal education has increasingly become the primary factor determining the scope for upward social mobility from one generation to the next.

Every complex society is characterized by stratification: the formation of social layers that differ in terms of power, property and prestige. A high position in one ranking order can enable people to improve their position in the others through 'status conversion'. Social mobility from one layer to another is something that occurs largely in societies with a less rigid and sharply defined stratification.

5 Relations between men and women

Early social science paid little attention to the special position occupied by women in society. Research was regarded as men's work and there was a tendency to speak of people in general without looking at the specific conditions of women's lives. Clearly, social science is itself afflicted by the short-sightedness and prejudices it sets out to study in others. This relative neglect of women has been much improved over the past few decades, and this too has been caused by social factors: more girls attend school than in the past, more young women are employed outside the home, and more study and teach at university, particularly in social science. All these developments have heightened interest in women's position in society, especially among researchers.

Unequal social relations exist between men and women. The inherent sexual differences are moulded socially into gender differences that vary from one society to the next. However, the differences between the positions occupied by men and women are related not only to gender but also to the position occupied by a woman's parents or husband. A woman attached by birth or marriage to a prominent man may be held in higher regard, be wealthier and have a stronger position of power than a man from a humbler background – the managing director's wife may be driven about by a chauffeur. At the same time, she will be held in less high regard, will have less property and less power than most of the men in her surroundings. Thus men and women do not constitute two separate social layers; within each layer, in all kinds of social surroundings, in every family, there is a large chance that the women will be at a disadvantage relative to the men. This gap is closing in present-day Western societies.

The main factor determining relations between men and women is a division of labour that may derive from conditions in nomadic societies, where a difference in physical strength was decisive in hunting and war. Pregnancy and the nursing of infants were particular impediments. The greater the threat of war, the more likely men were to claim a stronger power position, as warriors, *vis-à-vis* women. This threat of war was often bound up with the pressure of population – a scarcity of hunting-grounds and hence of food. To curb population growth, it was more effective to limit the number of girls, which explains the preferential treatment of boys in societies where food is scarce. Once established, relations persist long after the conditions that shaped them have ceased to apply. The inequality between men and women was often depicted in – and hence perpetuated by – religious images (although religions would often forbid the abuse of women by men, which had been a common practice before). In prosperous and peaceful societies, the inequalities in relations between men and women in general and between husbands and wives in particular gradually become less pronounced.

In modern times, war does not necessarily exacerbate the inequalities between men and women. In industrial societies in Europe, in wartime women took over jobs that had been exclusively reserved for men in peacetime, and after the end of the war they often stayed on. Today, sophisticated weaponry makes physical strength far less important than it used to be for a soldier, and women are now taking an increasing number of positions in the forces.

6 Old and young

There is another distinction that is primarily biological but is also in part socially formed – the difference between young and old. Young people are generally held in less esteem, have less property and occupy weaker positions of power than those who are more advanced in years. The *generations* (age groups) do not constitute a separate social layer in contemporary societies: rather, within each social group, in every family, there is an inequality between young and old. But young people grow older, and although unequal age relations change very slowly in society at large, they pass with aging in every human life.

A generation may be looked upon not only as an age group but as a 'birth cohort', the set of people who were born in a particular period. People who were born during the First World War were adolescents in the Great Depression and young adults during the Second World War. The children born in the post-war baby boom reached puberty in a period that witnessed a rapid growth in prosperity. These historical conditions make up the background of the lives of all those belonging to a particular cohort. The generation born in the 1950s is sometimes described as having enjoyed all the benefits of peace and prosperity; they now occupy the best positions and tend to exclude the following cohort. Today, the cohorts of the 1970s and 1980s are seeking grants, jobs and homes.

7   Established groups and newcomers

People who live in the same society as their parents and grandparents before them usually have an advantage over those who have just moved in. As a rule, the available jobs and homes have been divided up among the established inhabitants and the newcomers have to take whatever is left. Those who are already established have been building up their shared networks all their lives, and have numerous connections within them, whereas newcomers have yet to begin: their first contacts are generally with other people from the same country who arrived a little earlier.

If the housing and employment conditions are favourable, the newcomers find homes and jobs, they are absorbed into the neighbourhood and accepted by their fellow workers, and become increasingly involved in the new society. Their children grow up there and their grandchildren will eventually join the ranks of the established classes.

If employment and housing are scarce, however, the estab-

lished inhabitants have a tendency to close ranks and preserve what jobs and homes there are for themselves. In order
to achieve this *exclusion* the differences between established
people and newcomers are exaggerated. The outsiders are
perceived as different, inferior, less worthy: 'they simply
don't deserve' to be accepted into the new environment. The
newcomers have to go to the very end of the queue and put
up with the worst sort of accommodation and the least
attractive jobs. They are assigned to the lowest positions
because of their origins; the better positions are out of their
reach, regardless of their achievements. Their children may
well lose the expectation that education will provide access
to better-paid jobs and leave school without qualifications.

Excluded by the established inhabitants, the newcomers
strengthen their mutual ties and increasingly cherish the
customs and views of their country of origin: they too close
ranks. To the established inhabitants this reinforces the
perception of difference they had already come to emphasize.
The gap between the two groups widens and the mutual
expectations are confirmed. Hence a difference that perhaps
seemed transitory at the outset may harden: even when the
newcomers' descendants have been established for generations, they remain outsiders who occupy low positions in
every ranking order. This exclusion is all the more obdurate
if the outsiders are easily recognizable – by their skin colour,
height, attire or religious customs.

The Africans who were shipped to America became newcomers against their will, the lowest of the low in the rigid
and sharply delineated stratification of the slave society.
After the abolition of slavery they became tenant farmers or
acquired small farms of their own. During the Great
Depression they gravitated to the industrial cities of the
North, where they were newcomers again and once more
sent to the very back of the queue. In that disadvantaged
position they were highly recognizable by their skin colour.
A considerable proportion of African–Americans have
remained outsiders in North American society. Similarly, the
native inhabitants of former colonies who have settled in the

cities of Western Europe are newcomers who have difficulty gaining access to good jobs and houses. If this exclusion persists, there is a danger that later generations too may be outsiders, all the more identifiable as such by the colour of their skin. But skin colour is a secondary factor. What matters is the exclusion of newcomers that continues to apply to their descendants. Their outward characteristics come to be seen as marks of an inferior position. This is hence another instance of an innate difference being socially formed, because of people's expectations of one another.

5

How People Form One Another: Socialization and Civilization

Society continues to exist, while the people who are part of it die, and others take their places. The newcomers have to be formed to occupy their positions. This is done through *socialization*. In the long term, society as a whole changes too. In certain circumstances this involves a process of *civilization*.

1 The social formation of inborn abilities

People have much to learn, and much to unlearn, to be capable of social interaction. This learning process begins at birth, when a new person enters society. A baby needs no instruction to suck its mother's milk or to clutch someone. These are inborn reflexes. From the very first moment, the infant is fed, washed, changed, picked up, rocked, cuddled and stroked, and it hears a constant stream of words and noises. It soon responds to all that attention, first with vague sounds and movements, but gradually with clearer signals.

This process is easy to follow by watching the development of the *smile*. A small baby starts by making involuntary movements of the mouth, movements that do not really mean anything at all. But people looking into the cot think they see a smile and respond with high-pitched sounds and endearments. After a while the baby responds with specific movements of the mouth muscles, expressing contentment and recognition – signals. These are acknowledged by the people the baby sees, with cries and caresses. After three or four months the infant learns how to smile, but mainly at familiar faces and only in pleasant situations. In the first few years of life, children go on to build up a whole repertoire of faint smiles, grins and beams, with which they can express their emotions and desires quite accurately in all kinds of circumstances. And all the while they are also learning how to interpret the facial expressions of other people.

Everyone is born with the ability to curve the corners of the mouth into a smile. All vertebrates have the muscles needed to do this. Many animals pull back their lips and expose their – frequently terrifying – teeth as a threat and a warning. It is possible that this threat acquired a different function in some species in the course of evolution, becoming a sign of peaceful intentions, a greeting: 'I could bite you but I won't, because I have no desire to fight you.' In human children this inborn ability to bare the teeth becomes more and more refined, expanding into a whole range of signals, each of which has a meaning of its own and goes with a particular situation.

What this means is that people learn to make the right face to suit every situation. In this sense, all facial expressions are made and acted out, although there is rarely any conscious thought involved.

The learning process human children undergo in their interaction with others largely consists of expanding and refining inborn abilities. They learn an incredibly varied repertoire of types of behaviour, each action suited to a particular context. Children start by learning to crawl, then to walk upright, to run and jump, stamp and kick, stride, shuffle, hop and dance. In each situation a certain kind of movement is appropriate and others are out of place. Children are born with everything they need to walk, but they still have to learn this skill from others, in all sorts of variations, just as they have to unlearn everything that is considered improper.

Everyone learns how to walk, very many people also learn how to run and dance, but few progress to become professional dancers or athletes, devoting much of their lives to a specialized art of movement.

The entire learning process in which a human child develops into a competent member of society is known as *socialization*. This includes the acquisition of knowledge, skills, views and attitudes.

The most important thing of all is learning a language. The same applies here as to walking: human children are born with the apparatus they need to talk, including a speech centre in the brain, an extremely complex muscular system controlling the larynx, tongue and lips, as well as auditory organs, with which they can hear what other people are saying. This apparatus is suitable for the learning the language spoken all around them, their 'mother tongue' – one of the 5,000-odd human languages that are spoken on earth. And here too the repertoire is expanded and refined, from the first vague sounds to the mastery of a vast vocabulary and a complex grammar and syntax, enabling them to say the right thing in any situation. Again, part of this learning process is unlearning everything that is considered incorrect or improper, such as lisping, stammering, spitting, cursing, talking gibberish, and so on. Mastering a language means mastering yourself – it is yet another form of self-coercion and self-direction, and here too, the help of others is indispensable.

What children learn lies ready and waiting for them in their environment. Most of it is impressed on them by the people around them and in some cases actually imposed on them. They enter a social world that is already crammed full of knowledge, opinions, and ways of doing things. They must learn a whole range of social skills and attitudes until these become 'second nature', part of themselves.

Human children are more helpless at birth than the young of other species. They are extremely dependent on their carers and they can and must learn much more than other young animals. They also go on learning for much longer.

As they are so dependent and have so much to learn, people are more changeable than other species. They differ more from each other and from their parents and ancestors than other animals. Their patterns of behaviour are not fixed at birth, but can and must be formed. For this reason, human societies are more changeable and more diverse than other animals' social arrangements.

2 Socialization as a learning process

What would happen if children were not brought up and taught at all, but grew up entirely without human company? They would die. A few cases are known of children growing up 'in the wild' and surviving, but when found they were filthy and 'bestialized', they could scarcely walk and could not talk at all, and they never caught up.

Protection

Small children obviously need food and shelter. Equally obvious is their need for protection. Predators and thieves – *macroparasites* – are not the primary threat in modern societies. But household appliances, cleaning products and above all road traffic pose a constant threat to small children, which is why they are almost never allowed to roam freely. There is another danger threatening small children in densely populated areas: infection by *microparasites* such as viruses and bacteria. *Child mortality* has declined sharply over the past 150 years, above all through better housing, through houses being connected to the water mains and sewers, and better controls on food and drink, especially milk.

Knowledge

Socialization takes place in the family and among playmates, more or less casually and 'informally'. This is how children automatically learn to walk, talk and play and to acquire all the rest of the knowledge and skills that we completely take for granted. But knowledge is also imparted 'formally', at school, according to a fixed schedule and a regular curriculum, with tests, exams and certificates.

What children have to learn depends on the society in which they grow up. Knowledge acquired at school is more important today than it used to be. Children attend school in larger numbers and stay on longer. But in modern industrial societies some kinds of knowledge are no longer taught. People no longer know how to bake their own bread or kill a chicken, as there are bakeries and slaughterhouses to do it for them (and people flinch from killing an animal they are happy to eat, preferring not to think about that aspect of their food; human sensitivities have evidently changed too).

But even within a single society and in the same period the socialization process is different from one milieu to the next. In the fifteenth century, say, a young nobleman had to learn how to ride, fence, hunt and dance, a merchant's son was expected to master calculations and bookkeeping, while a peasant's son had to learn how to handle the livestock, the plough and the scythe. Girls were expected to master a different range of skills altogether. Even in modern societies, more girls than boys study foreign languages, while the opposite is true of mathematics and physics. It is still true today that the children of highly educated parents study longer than those of people with little schooling. The difference in education is hence 'hereditary', that is, 'socially inherited', passed on to children by parental influence. Social differences evidently make themselves felt in the transfer of knowledge and the socialization process in general.

Affection

From the moment they are born, children also need affection. If they do not receive enough love and attention they become ill. An experiment in which young monkeys were kept in complete isolation for a few months and fed but given no affection whatsoever revealed that they became utterly confused and were later unable to raise their own young. Where human children are concerned, it is generally accepted that early neglect can lead to emotional problems in later life and an incapacity to form intimate ties. Children who are raised with loving care, on the other hand, learn to become emotionally attached to those who love them, and as adults they are better able to maintain emotional ties. We know more about disturbed than about healthy emotional development. Social workers often have to deal with problem families, but researchers do not find it easy to gain access to families in which there are no problems.

Direction

Socialization includes modes of controlling or directing one's actions. Young children learn to control their bowel movements. They can only let them go in one special place, on their potty, and they learn to hold their water in bed at night. In some societies this *toilet training* is imposed at a very early age, quite strictly and sometimes heavy-handedly. In others the whole subject is approached more slowly and gently. These differences in toilet training are sometimes linked to differences in *personality formation*. In a society that tends to impose an iron discipline on bowel movements people are said to develop rigid, closed personalities, whereas a milder and more patient approach to toilet training supposedly leads to more flexible and spontaneous personalities.

Appetite is another thing that children have to learn to regulate according to the time of day – 'mealtimes'. They have to learn how to get through the day without too many sweets and snacks. In mastering *table manners* they have to unlearn all the other ways of putting food into their mouths. Some types of food are not allowed, while there are others they have to learn to eat. And no one who has been a child needs to be told that all that socialization means quite a struggle between children and parents, disagreements about what children should learn or unlearn, and also about what they are not allowed to learn.

Children learn to mind their language and are forbidden to use *dirty* words (which they have apparently learned) or to swear. They are taught to greet people politely and say please and thank you. They are also taught to dress properly and cover their nakedness, or 'they should be ashamed of themselves' – they learn this too, apparently.

Parents, brothers and sisters constantly use their powers of persuasion with small children, this persuasion ranging from explanations, compliments and 'setting a good example' to jokes and ridicule and sometimes scolding and punishment. This external pressure is primarily aimed at teaching the child to direct its own actions. Children are under *external coercion to coerce themselves*. A child eventually absorbs the rules it is taught by the people in and around its home so that they become its own beliefs. This process of *internalization* means that something originally presented as an external rule comes to be felt by the child as part of itself. This means that the child will be more inclined to keep to it voluntarily. The balance shifts from external coercion to more 'self-coercion'.

In present-day society, many people bringing up and educating children try more than in the past to explain and persuade instead of dishing out pure coercion through punishment and reward. With this social coercion they help to develop a process of self-coercion, so that children learn to direct their own actions at an early age. In families or school classes that work in this way it may seem as though 'anything goes', but in fact the children are under great pressure to conform.

Even when no one is looking, children and adults often keep to the rules. They feel obliged to do so, and would be ashamed to be found out if they went 'astray'. They even feel guilty if no one finds out. 'Shame' is something you feel when you imagine what others will think of you, whereas 'guilt' is something you feel when you think of what you have done to someone else.

Things that people regard as highly personal have nevertheless grown in the process of interaction with others. Each of us lives within the present and within reality, with the people who exist here and now. These are *actual relationships*. At the same time, we also live with memories of past relationships and with fantasies and expectations about possible and future ones. These are the *virtual relationships* within which someone lives. When the 'social' aspects of a human life are referred to, it is usually the person's actual relationships that are meant. When the 'psychological' aspects are mentioned, the focus is generally on a person's virtual relationships. And yet these virtual relationships, which exist in someone's imagination and memory, are social as well. They have to do with other people, and they have been formed in relations with others. By the same token, it is impossible to understand how someone responds to actual relationships without knowing anything about the person's virtual relationships.

3   Civilization

Societies too change over time. Medieval Europe was torn by constant struggle between overlords. Plundering and looting armies roamed through large areas of the continent. Peace was fragile, and in wartime life was cheap. In this age, what a lord needed, above all, was courage and heroism. It was a violent society in which there was often a stark choice between destroying or being destroyed. The strongest could do as they wished, and their weaker brethren simply had to accept it.

Things would only change when a lord managed to subject the warring parties in a very large region to his authority. Then society would gradually become more peaceful. People no longer needed to take up arms at a moment's notice; in fact they were forbidden to do so, as only the ruler and his men would be permitted to use force.

The qualities needed at the sovereign's court were very

different from those that would prevail on the battlefield. Here the accent was on courtesy, etiquette, eloquence and a talent for intrigue, diplomacy or government. Anyone who grabbed his sword at the least provocation would soon find himself out in the cold. In upbringing and education too, the emphasis shifted away from bravery and physical strength towards self-control and the observance of etiquette, good taste, consultation and regulation. And what was good form at court filtered down to the bourgeoisie, who took their behavioural cue from those who were one step higher up the social ladder than themselves. In the nineteenth and twentieth centuries these codes of conduct were adopted in part by the tradespeople and working classes. Education, which was increasingly accessible to them, played a large role here, and the labour movement also added a certain discipline.

This development in society towards more refined, more varied rules of conduct is known as the *civilization process*. As civilization becomes more firmly anchored in a society, different demands are made of the people who live there. They no longer need to be as courageous and eager to fight as in societies where violence can break out at any moment. But this also means that they have to learn to suppress their desire to fight, to keep their hands to themselves, and to watch their language. They learn to project the consequences of their behaviour into the future, and to take more account of other people. This means following their impulses less, and instead considering the consequences of their actions. They have to be able to do this without constantly being pressured to do so from the outside. They must be capable of directing themselves, with more accuracy and agility than was necessary in the past.

Today's technology makes similar demands. Anyone who succumbs to a fit of rage in traffic, for instance, is quite likely to cause a fatal accident. All those who take part in traffic learn to steer, brake and accelerate with great accuracy in order to negotiate a safe passage to their destination among other road users.

Much the same applies to financial matters. The more

extensive the use of money in a society, the more important it is for people to learn to deal with it in a controlled fashion. They cannot squander it, but must constantly bear in mind what they will need later. Workers used to be paid their wages weekly, and would have to make the money last until the following Saturday. Now monthly payment is the norm, and the income has to be spread over 30 days. But people also have to take account of large annual expenditures, such as holidays and tuition fees. Money concerns extend over an entire lifetime when it comes to paying for a house and contributing to a pension scheme.

So people very often have to defer the gratification of their needs. This applies just as much to children, who must learn from an early age to restrain themselves and modify their behaviour in preparation for their later studies and their career.

The gap between the highest and lowest layers of society has narrowed over the past few centuries. There is greater equality between people. This means that people in high places have to exercise more restraint in their dealings with those lower down the social scale. In the twentieth century the gap between men and women has narrowed a little, so that women now have more room to live their lives. The gap between parents and children, too, has narrowed. Parents take their children's wishes into account more than in the past, and children are less bound by their parents' authority.

Basically, the dominance of certain groups over others has lessened across the board, and the strict rules of the past are less absolute than they were. In other words, we have seen a shift from a system of management through *command* to one based on management through *negotiation*. People do not constantly have to follow rules and commands, and can more often decide in mutual consultation how they will deal with one another.

In relatively peaceful and prosperous societies, socialization places a heavy emphasis on inculcating knowledge and 'self-direction'. In other societies, in which violence and poverty have halted the civilization process, socialization too will move at a different pace. The focus on knowledge and self-direction in today's society has to do with the way in which the civilization process has developed: people are expected to practise a very strong, consistent and sustained self-direction.

The civilization process is not in any sense complete; it is going on all the time. But within every civilization process there are also counter-movements among certain groups or in certain aspects of society. The civilization process can sometimes go off on an entirely different track, especially in societies with increasing levels of violence, in which people are no longer confident that they will be protected from violence by their fellow human beings. Then the process may turn into *decivilization*.

6

What People Believe, Know and Think: Orientation

A large library contains many millions of books. There they are, stretching away for mile after mile, shelf upon shelf, bookcase after bookcase, row after row, room after room, each one neatly stacked away. Each one contains references to previous volumes, in footnotes, quotations or allusions. You could tie threads from one book to the next, right across the library's aisles and rooms, to show these connections. Gradually a fabric comprising tens of millions of threads would be created, spinning a web that would stretch to every corner of the entire library, its knots and twists quite impossible to disentangle. When you reach the oldest books of all, which are not printed but hand-written, the thread comes to an end. Rather than referring to older books they contain in writing the knowledge that had previously been passed on by word of mouth.

Even today, some societies have no written language; they are peoples of memory. They remember their stories and the older members of society pass them on to the younger ones, in a chain of oral tradition. What other societies commit to paper, they retain in their minds. All their stories, too, could be woven into the vast imaginary web.

This fabric of writings and oral tradition can be expanded still further. Sculptures and paintings often depict what was once expressed in words, in folk tales and ancient writings. Chants, music and dance are again adaptations of older sounds and movements, evoking what others have conveyed with words and images. The web now becomes almost infinite and defies imagination; it is a fabric as long and as complex as humanity itself.

People live in the mazes of that imaginary web, which has been spun by their predecessors and contemporaries and which they themselves elaborate. Only a tiny part of it is visible to them, and in that tiny part they follow a few lines, try to unravel the knots and to hold on to the thread. They set out to determine their own place and direction and to orient themselves in the web of the world. The fabric consists partly of images and notes, but most importantly of words: that is the web of language.

1 Language

In principle, everyone is capable of learning and using a language. We can gain a rough idea of how our ancestors lived together before languages were available to them by studying animals closely related to humans, such as chimpanzees. Like some other animal species they use sign systems, but they can only use them to transmit a very limited number of fixed messages. People can communicate an infinite number of different messages to one another. To do so, they draw on a vast vocabulary and apply linguistic rules to arrange the words into intelligible and well-formed sentences. Human languages were not invented or designed by anyone, they grew – and are still growing – in the course of time. Over hundreds, thousands of years, people have added countless expressions, which have gradually been absorbed into everyday language, while all sorts of words and phrases have gone out of use, and even some entire languages have become extinct.

Some languages, such as Dutch, Frisian and German, are quite similar. They are closely related, and derive from the same root language, which is no longer spoken. Russian, Latin, Persian, Hindustani and Dutch, on the other hand, appear to have little in common. Even so, they too have the same roots: all five are Indo-European languages.

Early farmers probably flocked into Europe from Asia Minor about 6,000 years ago, spreading their Indo-European *proto-language*, which developed and branched into the languages now spoken in the continent of Europe. Indo-European may even be related in a still more remote past to other language families, such as Amerindian, Austronesian and Sino-Japanese.

Even today, new languages are evolving while others are dying out. Sranan tongo, a Creole language spoken in Surinam, arose over the past few hundred years through contacts between the speakers of African languages, English and Dutch. On the other hand, Manx, an old Celtic language once spoken on the Isle of Man, is now extinct. Over the past four centuries, a number of languages have spread throughout the world as a result of the conquests made by the European powers in Asia, Africa and the Americas. French, Spanish and above all English are still spoken in these former colonies. English has increasingly become the language in which people with different native languages communicate worldwide.

Without language people can scarcely think, and without language contact between people is scarcely possible. So language is absolutely essential to human interaction. The development, spread and acquisition of languages are also examples of social processes. Not a word can be spoken without people. Language exists and endures in and through them; it is they who make, preserve and change it. A few inventors have designed new languages, orators and authors have enriched languages, official agencies proclaim linguistic rules and schools impose standard versions. But the development of a language is an example of a 'blind process' that was not invented or desired by anyone, but which comes about unintentionally through interaction between people, without them intending or even realizing it.

Language, then, is something people make and speak with each other, hear from each other, write for each other and read from each other. Within a language community people learn it from each other, adopt new words and expressions and sometimes forget old ones. Language continues to exist because it is constantly spoken and heard, written and read. Language is available in a society, without being located anywhere or in anybody. Almost all human beings know enough words and rules to be able to say whatever they want, yet no one knows all the words and rules of his or her own language. It is possible to formulate a sentence that someone else will understand without ever having heard it before (this sentence, for example!). It is even possible to think up a sentence that has never been said by anyone before, and that everyone will nonetheless immediately understand. (What would such a sentence look like?) If you want what you say to make sense to others, you have to use words and apply rules that exist in the common language; otherwise you will produce 'non-sense'. (And nonsense sentences too are easy enough to think up.)

Language use reflects much of the way in which people live their lives together. In China, rice has long been the most important food, and silk is a highly desirable material. So it is hardly surprising that Chinese has at least nineteen words for silk and eight for rice. In modern societies people know scores of names for types and makes of cars. Different groups within a society will each develop their own particular linguistic usage. Law graduates distinguish at least a dozen different legal rules, all of which lay people refer to as 'laws'. Skateboarders and surfers have specific names for manoeuvres that ordinary passers-by simply call 'tricks'. People make these distinctions and find new words for them as they go along, and it becomes easier to distinguish things more precisely once there are so many different terms for them. In this sense, each language influences the perceptions and actions of the people who think and speak in it.

Clearly audible variations in language use occur from one region to the next. If the speakers of these different regional forms can understand one another, we speak of *dialects*, local variants of a single language. Some centuries ago, these differences were far greater than they are today. The introduction of the printing press made it possible to distribute thousands of copies of all sorts of texts – in the West particularly the Bible – and to standardize the written language. This standard language was taught to children at primary school, other variants and accents being regarded as 'vulgar', 'uncouth' or 'uncivilized'. Today, this situation has been reversed to some extent. Thirty years ago, BBC newsreaders on national television were recognizable by their 'BBC English', the national standard. But today, Scottish, Welsh and Northern Irish accents have equal status (or ostensibly so) and newsreaders have a variety of accents. Minor dialects have suffered, however, through a certain standardization of language imposed by the media.

Language usage is influenced by social status as well as geographical location. A *sociolect* is a variety current in certain social circles. Many dialects are also sociolects: Cockney and Scouse are largely spoken in old working-class neighbourhoods. But many people are capable of switching from one language variant to another to suit the occasion. The standard language evidently confers greater status, whereas regional or group varieties strengthen the sense of group identity and solidarity with relatives or peers.

In most Western countries new sociolects develop when immigrants import accents, words and phrases from their own language into that of their adopted country. In the UK, for instance, we can now distinguish Jamaican and Trinidadian, Indian and Pakistani, Nigerian, Ghanaian and many other varieties of English. The children of these immigrants learn English at an early age (usually alongside their parents' language) and adopt a variant of English to use at home and among other members of their ethnic group.

2 Religion

People ask themselves all sorts of questions about the origins and the true nature of the world, life on earth, and humanity.

Surely there must have been a beginning, and there must be an end? Surely something, or someone, must have created the world, and the plants and animals and people in it? What is the meaning of life? How should people behave towards each other, and towards these higher beings? Is there some way to placate these higher beings, to gain their help and protection under difficult circumstances, and to avoid making them angry? What comes after death? Why is there injustice and misery in the world?

A system of explanations and customs that relates to questions of this kind is called a *religion*. At the heart of religious practice are rituals and ceremonies. They mark the days and the seasons, the transition from one phase of life to the next, the great events of social life. Religion imposes order on people's lives and on the history of their society. Religion gives meaning to events that are impossible to understand, it imposes a pattern, and may provide comfort in times of adversity. Religion also strengthens the sense of solidarity within society, provided that the believers have the same beliefs. Conflicts in which religious differences play a part are often the fiercest of all. When people are overwhelmed by the immediate threats posed by their physical and social surroundings, they are more likely to seek supernatural remedies and to try magic charms and spells to ward off disaster and to achieve their desires than when they are living in relatively protected circumstances.

There are many religions on earth, some of which are extremely old and have a great many adherents. Religion, too, is available within a society but does not exist in a specific place or person. It is a set of teachings and a practice that people interpret and pass on to each other. A religion always contains an explanation for human existence, for instance through revelation, inspiration or prophecy. But this religious message is distributed in a social process, first of all by parents passing it on to children, and secondly by people who are able to persuade and convert others. New elements are sometimes added to a religion's explanations and customs, while others pass into disuse. Then again, some religions grow out of others: Christianity arose from Judaism (which grew out of older religions) and Islam arose out of Judaeo-Christian tradition, while Protestantism developed from a split within the Catholic Church. More or less separately from this tradition, Hinduism and Buddhism developed in India, while China and Japan saw the emergence of Taoism and Shintoism, which influenced one another.

All these faiths have their 'religious specialists', people who have received a special education and consecration in a religion and who give lay people the benefit of their special expertise. In early agricultural societies, a caste of these *priests* developed alongside that of warriors. Because of their special knowledge and skills they enjoyed more respect and authority than the 'laity'. After all, priests had at their disposal the most important means of orientation in their society. In ancient times it was the priests who knew most about the motions of the celestial bodies, enabling them to determine the time of year and also to ascertain whether the time was opportune for planting or sowing seed, whether the drought would soon be over, and whether the river would overflow its banks. They knew more than anyone else about the stories and customs of the society and were adept in the use of language (often a special liturgical language, as in the case of Latin). They were often the only people who could read and write. Priests were also healers. As they knew most about the supernatural, they could also reassure people, or indeed terrify them, and try to direct their behaviour in this way.

Priests initially concerned themselves with all areas of knowledge, from astronomy to medicine, from mathematics to law and historiography. All these subjects gradually developed into specialized fields, each with experts of its own. In the course of this process, religious explanations came to figure less prominently in the practice of the sciences, and society witnessed a 'scientification' of the prevailing world view. Still, when it comes to prescribing how people should live, religion and 'religious specialists' continue to play a prominent role in modern societies.

Religion endures in society partly because people believe in the ideas it preaches, and partly because they assume that other people believe them too. Priests consolidate and disseminate that belief among their fellows, who listen to them, because they have access to special knowledge (their 'means of orientation'), and because they occupy key positions in the community. With this specialist knowledge, priests may choose to support or to denounce their society's leaders. They may proclaim, or deny, that the sovereign is of divine descent, or enjoys divine grace. Religious premises may serve to strengthen positions of military and political power or to weaken them. Conversely, religious specialists can consolidate their positions if they can gain the support of those in power.

People tend to follow the religion that is available – or in some cases omnipresent – in their social milieu, but they also have their own ways of incorporating the religious explanations and customs, focusing on the words and images that are of primary importance to themselves. So religion, like language, is as personal as it is social. Furthermore, to its adherents, religion is not only human and social but also – and above all – spiritual, of a higher order and significance.

Every religion has a number of rules for human interaction. Sometimes these rules are elaborated in a highly complex and detailed system. Priests then become the interpreters of the law. They concern themselves with crime and punishment; with the rights of husband and wife in relation to one another, or of parents and children; with questions of ownership, such as who is entitled to the land and the harvest; and with the interpretation of agreements that people have made among themselves.

3 Law

Rules of law originate from religious commands and from traditions, from *customary law*. Some rules are found in almost all societies: for instance, if you kill another human being, you must pay the price. Sometimes the victim's relatives kill or maim the murderer or a member of his family (in a *vendetta*), sometimes the murderer or his family have to pay compensation. In societies in which the ruler maintains law and order, the perpetrator is brought to justice and punished 'in the name of the king', without the victim's family having any involvement in this punishment.

People may not cause bodily harm to others (whether by murder, assault or rape). They may not appropriate others' property (by robbery or theft). This rule presupposes that people own property and that it can be determined what belongs to whom: the *law of ownership* then applies. Even where only land and livestock are concerned, this may call for highly complex rules. In modern societies the complexities are multiplied. All the land, all the buildings and all the goods belong to someone (or to an organization, a 'legal person'). Even texts, images, trademarks and designs are the property of the maker, who possesses copyright, *intellectual property rights*, over them.

People must abide by their agreements and promises. This rule is particularly important in commerce. A simultaneous exchange – barter – is simple enough, but if either delivery or payment is deferred, the parties must be held to the agreement. Such cases are provided for by *contractual law*. In present-day societies countless agreements of this kind are concluded, in which one party does not have to keep to his or her part of the agreement for many years – sometimes for decades, as in the case of a mortgage or life insurance. And all that time, the contracting partners must have confidence in one another.

Between man and wife, parents and children, and between other relatives, questions arise concerning the division of an estate, inheritance, mutual care and authority. These matters are governed by *family law*. How should the family property be used or divided? Who inherits what when a relative dies? How should parents care for their children, and what form of care should children arrange for their ageing parents? Who exercises most authority in the home, and how compelling is that authority? Such questions first arise in agricultural societies, where people live off the land and where issues relating to the ownership and use of that land are therefore a matter of life and death.

It will be clear that the rules of law relate first and foremost to matters in which conflicts may arise between people. Indeed, the main point of the justice system is to prevent and resolve conflicts. Rules of law guide the expectations that people have of one another. In general, everyone expects other people to keep to the rules. This expectation is backed up by the expectation that anyone who breaks the rules will have a price to pay. Someone who expects that rule-breaking will be met with punishment is more likely to toe the line. Someone who expects that others will be punished for any transgression will therefore expect them to keep to the rules.

What this means is that rules of law create order in mutual expectations and prevent conflicts arising. Law strengthens the *confidence* that exists among people in a society. If a conflict or a lawsuit arises nonetheless, the rules of law can help resolve the case. The most important social function of laws is hence to resolve disputes without violence arising between the parties concerned.

But the dispensation and maintenance of law and order also require coercive measures with which to force people to keep to their agreements. This often necessitates the threat of force, and sometimes actual force. All regulated societies have an organization that maintains internal law and order and watches over external security, and that has the means to use force if need be. The authority that applies these legal rules is the *state*. In present-day societies the state itself is bound to keep to rules of law (such as the constitution and administrative law). Such a state is governed by the *rule of law*.

This collection of rules for human interaction – the law – has also grown in the course of thousands of years. Prophets or great lawgivers have sometimes proclaimed new rules or formulations, but in the main the law develops without anyone planning or designing it, from custom, according to tradition, in everyday practice and in the endless succession of judgments in disputes in which courts always examine previous applications of the law.

The dispensation of justice is based on existing rules. Legal scholars try to make these rules as consistent as possible, to remove inner contradictions and to derive new rules from existing ones. In studying each individual case, judges ascertain which rules are applicable and what judgment is therefore appropriate.

The law is also constantly undergoing renewal. Copyright, for instance, relates to intellectual property, and becomes far more important in an age in which texts and images can be reproduced at the drop of a hat. Do computer programs now merit protection as intellectual property? What are the criteria for a new program to be regarded as someone's own work?

Developments in society are evidently reflected in law, but equally, judgments handed down by courts of law affect social interaction. If computer programs are given solid legal protection, designers will be willing to invest substantially in new ones, as they will later be able to demand payment from those who use their property.

As the law is based on such long traditions and has grown into such a vast and intricate structure, with inner inconsistencies having to be avoided at every stage, its development has a dynamic force of its own. But it is always developments within society that make renewal essential and that determine the direction of change. Even the law, our system of justice, is not to be found 'somewhere', in a statute-book or at the Supreme Court. It is a corpus of rules of interaction that people observe (and sometimes transgress), so that you can say that people 'do each other justice'. This has to be determined afresh in each situation, and in the case of any disagreement there are specialists who determine the relevant facts and apply the legal provisions in a reasoned way. The rules of law also change the balance of power in society. They limit the power of those who are strong and/ or armed over the defenceless. Law strengthens the position of those who lawfully possess property – that is, owners (including, say, the designers of computer programs), but it also sets limits to people's rights over their property. For instance, landlords cannot evict their tenants at whim.

People learn the most important principles of the law as part of their socialization. Once they are familiar with them, they soon come to believe that they and other people should keep to them. Even if they do not expect to be punished, they almost always keep to the basic rules enforced by the justice system, that forbid them to kill, harm, rob or deceive other people. This is part of their *sense of justice*.

The development of the law involves a certain amount of rationalization – an increasing emphasis on establishing the true facts and on sound logic, regardless of the outcome and regardless of the interest an individual judge may have in the judgment. To ensure this, judges are made 'independent'. Their salary or promotion has as little as possible to do with the judgments they give. This is the social basis for the independence of courts and their judges.

4 Science

The same rationalization can be found in the development of scientific thought, which stands for strict reasoning applied to facts that have been established objectively. 'Objectivity' means that the observation does not depend on the observer's personal qualities or chance situation, but that anyone else in the same position who followed the same steps would observe the same facts. This 'interpersonal transferability' implies that the practice of science is a social process, something that takes place between people.

Yet this scientific process requires special social safeguards. People must be in a fairly secure situation before they can start investigating the facts and devising theories to explain them without worrying about the possible consequences of the outcome for themselves. Some scientific discoveries, such as the fact that the earth revolves around the sun (rather than the other way round), or that animal species (including human beings) have developed in the course of evolution caused huge shock waves in society.

Social science became a recognized academic discipline rather later than the natural sciences and the humanities. This is partly because of society's dislike of making the relations between human beings, which appear to have been ordained from on high or in any case to be self-explanatory, the object of scientific inquiry.

The social sciences study human beings within the social arrangements which they together constitute. Social science is unlike other sciences in that its 'subjects' are themselves capable of learning what is said about them. Furthermore, people rightly assume that they know a great deal about human beings and societies without being professional researchers. The distinction between the social knowledge possessed by ordinary people and the scientific knowledge of society is not absolute, but a question of degree. The knowledge acquired in social science is wider and deeper than that possessed by ordinary people, as it is based on more numerous and more accurate observations and on systematic arguments. One special characteristic of social science is that experiments are virtually ruled out. What takes their place is the comparative analysis of different societies, studied over the course of time.

A new discovery in astronomy does not change the motions of the stars, but a discovery in social science may well bring about change in society. This is why people sometimes react very sharply to the results of research in the social sciences, as these may undermine or consolidate their own positions. This comes out most clearly in research into the differences between people, such as those between men and women, between homosexuals and heterosexuals, between dark-skinned and light-skinned people. If one group appears to do better than another in some area of endeavour – in academic life or in the world of music, say, should this activity be reserved for them? If one group appears to be better than another at bringing up children, should this responsibility be theirs alone? Or should others be given extra practice in such skills, to compensate for their disadvantages? Are such differences inborn, or are they acquired in the course of social interaction? And if aggression, for instance, is an inborn tendency, can nothing be done about it? Or should those concerned be given careful guidance to control it? All these questions provoke fierce social debate, which is rekindled by every new pronouncement in social science.

Even the most innovative of discoveries does not appear out of the blue. It derives from existing knowledge, adding a new fact or a surprising perspective. No one can take in the entire field of science, or even a single discipline, yet all scientific knowledge is in principle available to everyone and intelligible to anyone who has sufficient basic knowledge in that field.

The close connections that exist between social science and the society around it mean that it is heavily influenced and distorted by its social context. There was once a National Socialist pseudo-science of society, and Communism too evolved its own phoney social science. These totalitarian regimes gave their scientists none of the social safeguards that would protect them from the consequences of their pronouncements. In democratic societies too, scientific funds, organizations commissioning research, sponsors and other funding agencies, the media and public opinion all exert constant pressure on the research community to do research with practical applications and to avoid unduly controversial conclusions.

5 The arts

People in all societies make music. They also dance, make sculptures and pictures, and tell stories. Such expressions often play a magical and ceremonial role in religion. In the course of time, the law, science and the arts have become more independent of religion: culture has become 'secularized'. The arts too have their own repertoire of forms and sounds, techniques and instruments, that are available in society. Writers, musicians and other artists in society build on these possibilities and are constantly contriving new ways of applying the available material. Art is not something that exists in any individual, nor does it exist outside people. Some works of art endure long after those who originally made and enjoyed them have vanished from the earth. This applies not only to stone statues and paintings, but also to written texts and compositions, and even to stories and songs that are passed on orally. Artists constantly seek to build on previous artistic expressions or rebel against them. Artistic development follows a path of its own. It derives from a long tradition, in which new elements are constantly being added. This is the 'creative' aspect of art. To contemporaries, innovations in the arts often appear very strange, but in the course of time it becomes clear that this avant-garde art is also a continuation of artistic traditions.

Artists often describe the creative process as something that is entirely unrelated to their teachers, fellow artists and clients, as pure 'inspiration'. Art lovers too prefer not to see their preferences in terms of the influence of prominent critics, respected acquaintances or the dominant style, taste and fashions of their time. They prefer to believe that their admiration has been aroused by the work of art itself, without any outside influence. After all, to be guided by something or someone else would make one a snob. True, someone who creates a work of art or who enjoys someone else's work has a sense of undergoing a direct, personal experience. Still, it can be shown that artists and art lovers take their cue from the standards of the marketplace and prevailing aesthetic norms. For the art-loving public it is also important that their familiarity with expressions of 'high' art enhances their *distinction*; it sets them apart from people unable to appreciate such art forms, who are therefore 'lower' down on the social scale. Familiarity with 'high' art thus enhances prestige. At the same time, people with the same artistic tastes develop a feeling of mutual solidarity. Works of art fulfil other functions too. They evoke emotions and aesthetic experience. These experiences too are embedded in society. Attending art classes, talking to other enthusiasts, reading reviews and listening to interviews all help to make people more receptive to various art forms. But this does not make their responses at all predictable or uniform. These responses 'have a life of their own', are aroused by specific works of art and occur in the individual emotional life of a specific person with a unique history.

Artists work for clients. In centuries gone by they worked for the Church, for those in power – they always rely on those who can afford to pay for their work. Nowadays they are often subsidized by the government or private foundations. In modern times vast numbers of people can become acquainted with the arts. Books can be published in large editions, colour prints make it possible for reproductions of paintings to be disseminated on a large scale, music can be broadcast on the radio and played on audio equipment, and dance performances, operas and plays have audiences of millions through film and television. For hundreds of years an art for connoisseurs, a 'high' form of art made and enjoyed at the court and in the capital cities, has coexisted alongside all sorts of folk art, which vary from one region to the next. With the advent of the mass media this folk art has gone into decline and is gradually being converted into commercial genres, 'low' forms of art with very wide appeal.

On the other hand, government and foundation grants have created a protected area within which artists focus less on the market, and more on the criteria set by highly skilled experts, so as to qualify for subsidies.

All the means of orientation that have been discussed here are part of *culture*. In the widest possible sense, culture means everything that people have added to their natural surroundings and passed on to subsequent generations – material objects as well as social customs and ideas. 'Culture' is hence opposed to 'nature'. Means of orientation belong to the customs and ideas of culture. In a rather narrower sense, the term applies primarily to a particular people or a particular group, as in 'French culture', 'courtly culture' or 'the rap subculture'. In colloquial language 'culture' is often understood in an even narrower sense, to mean the arts, the humanities and possibly science, or 'high' culture – Culture with a capital 'C'.

With language, religion, law, science and the arts, people try to orient themselves in human existence. None of these means of orientation exists completely within any one individual, nor do they have any existence outside people. They are available in society, by being stored in libraries, collections and museums, and most of all because people are actively involved in them, pick them up from others and pass them on. In this process people are constantly adding something of their own. Means of orientation are hence the result of social activities over very long periods of time. Usually they change gradually, and sometimes in fits and starts, but they develop in accordance with a dynamic force of their own, and retain their overall cohesion.

7

How People Attune their Efforts to One Another: Competition and Coordination

In order to survive, people depend upon one another in every way. Here we shall look at how these mutually dependent people attune their efforts to one another, so that the needs of one are fulfilled through cooperation with others. This is the issue of *coordination*. In the course of history, coordination has taken place on an ever larger scale, from small family groups to vast multinational states and even to a global society.

There are six different ways in which human beings coordinate their efforts: through family ties, reciprocity, collective action, market formation, organization and state power. This chapter will deal with the first two of these forms of collaboration, those based on family ties and reciprocity. The others will be dealt with in subsequent chapters.

1 The biology of cooperation: kinship and care

The natural world is marked by a constant struggle for survival. But it is not simply a struggle in which every creature is pitted against every other creature; to survive, cooperation is often indispensable. In the animal kingdom, and even more so in the world of human beings, competition and cooperation always occur together and in differing combinations.

Males of the same species compete with each other for the most eligible females, and vice versa. But once a female and a male have mated, in a great many species a cooperative phase begins, with the aim of ensuring the safe birth and upbringing of the new offspring. The parents feed and protect their young until they are big enough to take care of themselves and to reproduce. This requires an effort that they could have used to benefit themselves; instead, it benefits their offspring.

This behaviour is largely or wholly inscribed in genetic material, the *genes* that the parents carry within them and pass on to their young. Certain genes predispose their carriers to behave in certain ways. Suppose there was a gene that inclined its bearer to neglect its young. The offspring would soon perish. Not having any offspring themselves, they would not pass on the genes inherited from their parents. In other words, a gene leading to neglect will not be passed on to future generations. On the other hand, if there was a gene that predisposed its carrier to care adequately for its offspring, the latter would have a greater chance of survival and be more likely to reproduce. The 'good care gene' they inherited would be disseminated further, and subsequent generations would be cared for better still by parents likewise carrying the 'good care gene'. *In any one species the genes that become widely disseminated will be those that contribute to the carrier's suitability to reproduce more offspring with a greater chance of survival.*

This line of reasoning goes some way towards explaining why parents help their children to survive, and why, more generally, blood relatives tend to go to each other's assistance. For relatives have more identical genes than non-relatives. By helping each other, they increase the survival and reproduction chances of blood relatives that carry a type of gene they carry themselves, and thus improve the chances of its dissemination. A gene that inclines carriers to come to the aid of blood relatives will be disseminated more and more widely, as it will enhance the survival rate of other, related carriers, and will be passed on through them. A great deal of cooperation in the animal kingdom, and in the world of human beings too, takes place between close relatives. Where people are concerned, this form of cooperation takes place either in the nuclear or extended family or in *clans*. As shown above, people have a natural ability to help others to survive. But this biological account of the cooperation between blood relatives cannot explain coordination between non-relatives. It is typical of human beings that they do not confine their cooperative efforts to social arrangements of close relatives. This is yet another instance of a social learning process in which people modify and elaborate a potential inherited though their genes. This learning process is part of the socialization that takes place in the life of every individual, and in the course of history it takes the form of the development of societies, through collective action, market formation, organization and state formation.

People have taken to forming ever larger survival units. In the nomadic phase, a survival unit would comprise a few dozen people, all of whom would be closely related. At the dawn of agricultural society, each settlement would perhaps number a few hundred people, but in the course of time enormous empires developed, containing hundreds of thousands or even millions of people. Industrial societies are organized into states with tens of millions of people. Over the past two centuries, multinational states have arisen, capable of coordinating many hundreds of millions of people quite effectively: the United States, the Soviet Union, India and China. Sometimes, however, such superstates collapse, as in the case of the Soviet Union.

2 The sociology of cooperation: reciprocal obligations

When two parties cooperate, it is always clear which of the two has already done something for the other, and which still owes something in return. But if there is only one meeting, a problem arises. How do you know that your well-meaning gesture will elicit a similar response? The other may disappear without reciprocating. So you may decide it is better not to take the risk, in which case no cooperation will develop. If there is to be another meeting, however, you may well take the risk. In this case, any omission of a reciprocal gesture would rebound upon itself, as you would hardly be inclined to make a further advance on cooperation. The other party understands this, and will therefore be willing to make a reciprocal gesture at the start.

An important – negative – type of cooperation is an agreement not to attack. In societies that have not yet been pacified – in other words, that lack a government that is able and willing to maintain the peace, by force if need be – strangers initially mistrust each other. One may be out to destroy the other – 'you never know'. We are familiar with this kind of meeting, full of suspicion, from Westerns, which depict life in the 'Wild West' when the army and the police had not yet fully established law and order. If both parties expect to meet again, they will be more likely to risk a friendly gesture, since they can always retaliate later on if swindled or robbed. People who associate regularly over a period of time are far more willing to cooperate, and mistrust each other far less, as all those involved know that there will always be another opportunity to reward someone's help or to punish their omissions.

This mutual trust can be of great benefit to society. In societies that are relatively unfamiliar with commerce and credit, people often fail to honour their debts. Commercial networks scarcely exist, and there is little chance of the debtor doing business with the same person again. And since so many people so frequently default on their obligations, few will be found willing to make loans or to supply goods in advance of payment. As a result, trade does not pick up momentum. Clearly, trade at a distance and with a time lag is a matter of trust. However, sometimes a small group of trading people settle in such a society – people who *have* built up a commercial tradition and who have learnt to trust each other, partly because they are related, speak the same language, practise the same religion, observe the same customs and come from the same region. This small community has an advantage, as its members can give each other credit and agree on future deliveries. Such *trading minorities* have often proved extremely successful: they include the Armenians and Jews in Europe, the Chinese in what is now Indonesia, the Indians in Africa and the Lebanese in Latin America.

One of the most general rules of conduct between people is that of *reciprocal obligation*:

> '*You must help someone who has helped you; and you may not harm someone who has helped you.*'

This rule only becomes common currency – and only works – in social arrangements in which people frequently meet each other. Complete strangers, who may never see each other again and need not fear any reprisals, will be far less trusting. In a system of reciprocal obligations, for instance, it is customary to present a gift on a solemn occasion. This puts the recipient under an obligation to refrain from harming the givers and to present a gift of equal value on a subsequent occasion. Neighbourly help is another example. Your neighbours may help you at harvest time, or lend a hand when you are putting up a shed, and you are then under an obligation to help in return when the occasion arises, and meanwhile not to harm your benefactors in any way.

Mutual assistance and the exchange of gifts still exist in modern societies: students help each other to move house, friends bring snacks and wine when someone has a party, and people give their friends and relatives birthday presents. Without saying so in so many words, people generally remember very well what they have given someone, and what they have received. And they retain the sense of owing the giver or helper 'something in return'; or alternatively, of being owed something by someone they have helped or given something. Because of this, many people feel uncomfortable if they receive a valuable present or if someone does them a huge favour. Something has to be given in return, and some may find this sense of obligation so oppressive that they would rather not ask for help at all, and prefer not to receive presents. They do not want to be in anyone's debt. In a system of reciprocal obligations, then, all the parties involved keep a kind of record at the back of their mind in which they balance debts and claims. They also have to have roughly similar ideas about what services and gifts are equivalent, so that they will agree when they are 'even'. If this system breaks down, a quarrel ensues – and in fact it frequently does. Moreover, the system does not work in larger circles, or between people who do not meet on a regular basis. In these situations, debts and obligations are settled straight away. If you stand a round of drinks at the pub, your companions are each under an obligation to pay for a subsequent round. Among 'regulars' however, this is not essential, because there will always be another occasion on which the friends can return the favour.

The system of reciprocity works in modern societies without any coercion or law. If you have presented a gift, or provided help, and the other person does not feel like reciprocating, there is no point in calling the police or taking legal action. The system does not usually work with money. The neighbour, relative or friend who has helped or provided a gift is not paid; the other party is expected to do something in return.

Someone who fails to meet such an obligation may find that others are disinclined to help out the next time. People generally feel morally bound to meet their obligations, and they also fear the sanctions (punitive measures) that others may apply to them. Defaulters may find people gossiping about them, making fun of them, refusing to talk to them or even to say hello in the street, or excluding them from social relations altogether – *ostracizing* them. Persons targeted in this way suffer a loss of respect and affection. These measures are *informal social sanctions*, sanctions not based on laws or implemented by formal agencies, but applied locally within small groups to punish transgressions such as a failure to meet one's obligations.

3 Reciprocity between groups

Reciprocal obligations often exist between individuals, but they can also exist between groups, if in a slightly different form. When two groups of nomads meet in the wilderness, they will draw near with a degree of suspicion. Will the other side attack, or present gifts? An *exchange of gifts* is a way of ensuring that such a meeting proceeds without incident, which is in both parties' interests. The next step in such a *rapprochement* may be an exchange of marriage partners (mostly women). A man from one group marries a woman from the other, and vice versa. The foreign partner serves as a kind of hostage and the children create blood ties between the groups. Hence the exchange amounts to a peace treaty. It arouses an expectation of other equally peaceful meetings in the future. The exchange of gifts thus acts as a sort of barter trade, and is accompanied by plenty of show and ceremony, to emphasize the peaceful intentions on both sides. But the exchange of gifts and marriage partners may misfire, in which case war may ensue.

Noble families and royal courts also place themselves under reciprocal obligations by solemnly exchanging gifts and joining their houses in marriage. Even today, heads of state will bear gifts on official visits, exchange titles of great distinction and attend official banquets and gala performances to confirm their countries' friendly relations with the host nation.

This chapter has looked at cooperation between relatives and between two parties who are identifiable to one another. Coordination becomes far more difficult when someone's efforts do not benefit a blood relative or any identifiable party, but an entire group of people, who cannot be counted upon to do anything in return.

8

How People Perform Tasks Together: Collective Action

Sometimes people cooperate to achieve something that none of them could achieve individually and that benefits their entire group, including those who have not helped to bring it about. One person's use of it does not mean that anyone else has less of it, and no one can be excluded from it. This is known as a *collective good*, and this kind of cooperation is called *collective action*.

1 Dilemmas of collective action

Two thousand years ago, much of what is now the Netherlands was marshland or was regularly flooded by the sea. Even so, the land was inhabited; the people built their homes on man-made hills, or terps. They put their livestock out to graze on the surrounding land, but at high tide it was always flooded. They could reclaim the land by protecting it from the water with dikes. But this would call for a collaborative effort, since it was far too big a job for a family that inhabited a single terp; and anyway, it would have been very impractical to have a separate dike around each terp. Of course, the dike could still be built if some of the families did not join in. A dike around the entire area would protect everyone, including the families that had not contributed to the work. This made it very tempting to leave others to do the arduous work and to enjoy the fruits of it without having to bear the burden. The building of a dike, then, has all the characteristics of a collective good, and the cooperation needed for it has all the properties of collective action. But it took more than a thousand years for the dikes to be built. Why?

Strangely enough, the problem is precisely that the dike can be built without everyone taking part. Perhaps some terp families would sit back and watch while others did all the work. The dike would still be built, and they would benefit from it without having done a thing. You can hardly fix things so that only their field will be flooded.

As the terp-dwellers are not sure whether everyone will help, they remain mistrustful and reluctant to commit themselves. This is another example of interdependence, since whether the dike is built or not does not depend on any one individual, and whether someone's individual effort produces the desired result depends on the cooperation of others. Once again, it is a question of mutual expectations. One person anticipates that others may want to profit from his work without contributing anything, and therefore does nothing. The others are equally suspicious. Yet they would all far rather live behind a dike surrounded by fields that were not constantly being flooded. They face a difficult choice. They can decide to participate, in the hope that joint action will produce the dike, but taking the risk that so many others will not participate that their own efforts will be pointless. Alternatively, they can decide not to participate, in the hope that others will build the dike without them having to do anything, and that they will be able to pluck the fruits; however, there is a good chance that the others will reach the same conclusion, and nothing will be done. The difficult choice articulated here is the *dilemma of collective action*.

The dilemma of collective action

	They join in	They do not join in
I join in	The dike is built, partly through my efforts (2)	I work for nothing (4)
I don't join in	The dike is built, and I do nothing (1)	No dike, no work (3)

It appears that each person's decision is based not only on the desired goal, but also on an assessment of what others will do. The best outcome is if the dike is built without 'my' having to do anything (1). The next-best outcome is if the dike is built, even though 'I' have had to work on it (2). If the others do not join in it is better to follow suit, so nothing will be done (3). For if the others do not join in, and 'I' do make the effort, 'my' work is for nothing. That is the worst outcome of all (4).

What will the others think of this? They all harbour precisely the same suspicions, and so they each reach the same conclusion: it is best to do nothing. In this way the muddle continues as before. Yet there must be a way out of these paralysing dilemmas. After all, the dikes were eventually built, and countless other collective goods have been created.

2 Resolving the dilemmas: force

External force may provide a solution, and it is one that has often been used. Precisely how the dikes were eventually built in the terp region is not known. But let us imagine that a powerful ruler conquered the district. He might force the terp-dwellers to build the dikes, and let it be known that non-participants would be punished. That would change matters. It would no longer be so advantageous to have others do the work and to benefit from it without joining in, since this would mean incurring a severe penalty. In this situation too, all the terp-dwellers would be following the same line of reasoning. So now everyone would assume that each of the others would cooperate for fear of punishment, and this would dispel people's suspicions. Curiously enough, in this case the threat of punishment would result in the terp-dwellers doing precisely what they most wanted to do, but which they could not bring themselves to do while they were paralysed by mutual distrust.

Thus force may have a liberating effect, dispelling mutual suspicions. There are other examples of this mechanism. In nineteenth-century England, factory-owners often enforced working days of fourteen hours or longer. Some were afraid that this would eventually seriously undermine the health of the working classes. That would have an adverse effect on industrial production as a whole, which was certainly not in their interests. Factory-owners were therefore willing to cut working hours, but they were all afraid that their competitors would not do so, and would end up making more profit at their expense. This is why the more progressive English entrepreneurs did not protest when a law was introduced prescribing a shorter working day (although they wanted to be sure that the law would also be applied to their rivals). It was in the short-term interests of each individual factory-owner to have employees work long hours, but it was in all of their long-term interests, in a wider context, to ensure that the English working class would remain productive.

Another example. Some species of fish are nearing extinction through overfishing. Again, in the short term, each individual fisherman wants to arrive at market with the largest possible catch. But it is in the long-term interests of each one, and of all the fishermen collectively, to preserve the fishing stocks by means of fishing quotas. In this case too, they have to be able to rely on the quotas being enforced, by coercive measures such as controls and the punishment of offenders.

In the age of the terp-dwellers, there was no government,

nor any ruler who could successfully exert force. So why did the terp-dwellers not set up their own 'dike police' that could force all the terp groups to participate by threatening them with fines or some other punishment? Because a 'dike police' would itself be a collective good, from which all the terp groups would benefit and to which a number of them would have to contribute. Precisely the same problems that arose with the building of the dikes would also hamper the formation of a dike police.

3 Resolving the dilemmas: the assumption of cooperation

Yet people sometimes succeed in creating a collective good without any threat of force. To do so, they must first dispel the mutual distrust that can be so crippling. The dilemmas of collective action can also be resolved when it comes to be taken for granted, for whatever reason, that everyone will be willing to join in.

It often helps if there is some kind of shared agreement about how the work will be done, a sort of code of conduct that each person knows is known to all the others involved. Heavy snowfall makes it difficult for everyone to get around, so a clean street is a collective good. One sensible rule is for all the residents to sweep the path in front of their own houses. People assume that this rule is known and accepted by all. Each individual takes it for granted that others take it for granted too. Confident of this, all the people clear their own areas. If one person can't be bothered, it is glaringly obvious which section of the path has not been swept. The uncooperative neighbour too is aware of having violated a generally accepted rule. This is shameful, and shame is in itself a form of punishment. It is apparently helpful if everyone's share in the collective effort is visible to everyone else.

Collective action can also be engineered by the *manipulation of expectations*. A neighbourhood committee collects money for a street party and tells a shopkeeper that the others have already pledged a contribution. The shopkeeper then assumes that the party is likely to be a success and makes a contribution, partly for fear of standing out as a skinflint.

People often underestimate what it will cost them to take part in some collective action, or overestimate the usefulness of the end result. In this case collective action is set in motion by *illusions*. Strikers often underestimate the length of a strike and are overly optimistic about their chances of success. But precisely because their expectations are pitched too high, because of their illusions, each of them is more willing to cooperate, and a collective action is engineered that ends up being more beneficial, viewed in hindsight, than if they had not joined forces.

4 Collective action as a transitional phenomenon

Looked at more closely, the dilemmas of collective action are typical of a transitional phase. They arise when a number of individuals or groups already understand that they have similar problems that they cannot resolve on their own, that a collective solution exists and that they therefore need one another: they realize that they are *interdependent*. On the other hand, there is not yet any agency that can mediate between these fairly autonomous units and effectively coordinate their efforts. In other words, the units are already interdependent, and are aware of it, but they are not yet effectively coordinated. They do not yet constitute a *collectivity*.

It is often leaders who are able to engineer collective action, maybe because they are good at making a convincing case for the advantages of the collective good, because they present a rule for the division of labour that all the participants will endorse, or because they set up meetings, manipulate mutual expectations or are able to create shared illusions.

Once the individual units have embarked on collective action – in other words, once they start cooperating – a process of collectivization is initiated. It is from this cooperation that both the collectivity and the collective good result. It does not always work, but it has a fair chance of succeeding. While the project is in progress, people can check each other's efforts, they make rules for the division of tasks, and develop a sense of togetherness and solidarity. In short, they become a more and more tightly knit group. They gossip, criticize or ridicule those who fall behind and may even reject them. They practise on each other a form of social coercion leading to 'self-coercion'. To put it differently again, they apply informal social sanctions that work rather like fines. They make it less attractive to have others do the work and to enjoy the benefits afterwards.

Both the collective good and the effective collectivity are generated in the collectivization process. The transition from a collection of fairly autonomous but interdependent units to a larger group linked by effective coordination leads in this way to a higher *level of integration*.

In this process, each unit balances its various interests. On the one hand, there are limited and short-term interests, and on the other hand there are interests that apply in the longer term and within a wider context. The dilemmas of collective action arise in a transitional phase, when none of the units can be confident that the others will allow the longer term and the wider context to prevail.

The dilemmas may occur between individuals, between groups (the terp groups, for instance) or even between states, in issues such as disarmament and the environment.

In present-day society, most collective goods are brought about by forcing people to contribute to them. Citizens pay tax to the state – and it is compulsory to do so. The state uses taxes to create all sorts of collective goods. The building of dikes – a vital collective good in the Netherlands – has already been mentioned. The conservation of the environment is another example. If there is air pollution or water contamination, everyone suffers. Protecting the environment is therefore a collective good. National defence also comes under the heading of collective provisions. People do not contribute to these collective goods voluntarily. So there is no question of them waiting suspiciously to see if others will play their part. They are all liable to pay taxes, and share the costs in this way.

In most cases, a good may have both collective and individual aspects. It is in citizens' interests that their fellow citizens should be in good health, if only to minimize the risk of contagion. Partly for this reason, public health care has collective features. On the other hand, someone may separately undergo medical treatment. That is the individual aspect of health care. Something similar applies in the case of education. It is in everyone's interests for their fellow human beings to be able to speak, read and write the same language well, and for experts to be available in virtually every sector of human knowledge. Still, all people acquire knowledge in an individual process, and also derive individual benefit from their own knowledge and skills.

Nowadays people are less dependent than in the past on voluntary joint action to create collective goods, because the state pays for them out of the taxes it collects. At the level of integration of a national society, the state ensures effective coordination. When it comes to arranging matters between states, however, the dilemmas of collective action remain as acute as ever. States are interdependent in every way, as government leaders are well aware. Yet there is as yet no agency that can effectively coordinate cooperation between states – a sort of 'superstate'.

The process of collectivization helps to explain how people have gradually formed larger units of effective coordination in the course of time. But other processes have played their part as well, and it is these that will be addressed in the following chapters.

9

How People Produce for Others and Exchange Goods: Division of Labour, Market Formation and Payment

A single network connects people everywhere on earth in a thousand ways. This is the web of exchange relations, which collectively make up the global economic system. All the people in this network use things that they have not found, cultivated or made themselves, but have acquired from others in an exchange or purchase. Endless flows of goods traverse the world in ships, trucks, trains and aeroplanes, on their way from producers to consumers, from sellers to buyers. At the same time, invisible flows of money travel in the opposite direction as payment. But there is a two-way flow of traffic in goods, too. No country can keep importing goods and paying for them in money; eventually it will also have to export goods or services and receive money in return.

1 Division of labour

When something is to be exchanged, purchased or sold, the two parties evidently have something to offer each other. They do not make the same thing; each makes a particular product that can be exchanged for all sorts of other necessities. This diversity of productive activities is known as the *division of labour* within society. Exchange and the division of labour are related in two ways. You could choose to spend your entire life making a single product, but this will only work if the product can always be sold in order to acquire the other goods necessary for survival. Conversely, exchanges are only possible if other people are making and offering other products – that is, if the total production in society is divided into a large number of separate tasks, each of which is performed by different people.

In the course of history, an increasingly complex division of labour has evolved. In agricultural societies, the vast majority of the population work on the land. There is a division of tasks between men and women, between young and old, and often between landowners and landless journeymen. The yield from the land is divided up. The labourers are paid not in money, but in kind: they receive part of the harvest as their wages, or are permitted to work small pieces of land for themselves.

In a farming community, some people become craftsmen, devoting themselves to making farming tools: ploughwrights and smiths, potters and basket-weavers, cart-makers, thatchers, brickmakers, carpenters, masons and so on. Then there are other craftsmen who process the harvest – millers, bakers, spinners, weavers, painters, tailors, oil-pressers and rope-makers.

Specialists of this kind will obviously provide better products – and faster – than the farming families themselves, who would previously have made such items in the quiet winter months. The rise of specialized crafts increases the quantity and quality of products available. Craftsmen and farmers exchange crafted wares for raw materials. People are constantly using things they have bought or acquired through an exchange. Such goods embody not only the human labour with which they were made, but also a network of exchange relations. This book, for instance, is made of paper derived from wood from Norwegian(?) forests and processed in the United Kingdom(?), and printed with ink from dyes that may come from any number of regions. This simple example makes it clear that people need not know where or how an article was produced, what it is made of, or through what exchange network it reached them in order to use it. In fact, they are usually completely ignorant of such matters. In this sense, people in modern societies know less about the world around them than illiterate nomads know about their own surroundings.

The division of labour goes together with a *division of knowledge* in which each individual need possess only a tiny share of the vast quantity of knowledge available in society – what they need in their specific role as the maker of their own particular product (their 'professional knowledge') and what they need to be able to use the products made by others, and to act as a competent member of society in other ways (their 'lay knowledge').

2 Money

At least one member of each household is directly connected to the exchange network through the 'cash nexus', whether as a wage-earner, benefit recipient, pensioner, entrepreneur or shareholder. This was not always the case. Even in Europe, it has only been in the last few centuries that this network has become so all-pervasive. Market formation and the division of labour are related developments. The more people devote themselves to making a particular product or providing a particular service, the more dependent they are on the market, where they can obtain all the other goods and services they need in exchange for what they have to offer. In this exchange, *money* has come to play an increasingly essential role.

Money is first and foremost a *medium of exchange*. It facilitates exchanges. Where no money is in circulation, one person's needs have to correspond exactly to what another person has to offer. Someone who has a calf for sale, and needs two baskets and a plough, must find someone else who not only has these precise items for sale, but who also happens to need a calf. If no such person is to be found, the owner will have to chop the calf in two and sell the back half for the baskets and the front half for the plough. But if the calf can be sold for cash, the seller can spend some of the money at the basket-maker's and use the rest to buy a plough.

It also often happens that someone sells something, but wishes to postpone making a purchase. Meanwhile, the money is set aside, or hoarded; it serves as a means of *saving*.

Quite apart from any specific purchase or sale, the value of all sorts of goods and services can be calculated in terms of money. In this sense, money acts as a *measurement of value*. The value of almost everything – but not quite everything – may be expressed in terms of money. But sometimes an article's value in money is quite different from its utility value, and different again from its emotional value. For instance, someone may own a bicycle that serves him extremely well and that he certainly has no desire to sell for its market price. In this case, the utility value exceeds the value in money (the *exchange value*). Moreover, the bicycle may well be an heirloom that the owner 'would not part from for any amount of money'. What matters is the owner's emotional attachment to it.

In order to fulfil all its functions, money has to be made of *divisible* material. Furthermore, there must be no doubt that it is 'genuine'. This means it must be possible to *assay its composition*. The material also has to be *precious*, that is to say that a small amount will buy a lot of goods. Finally, the material has to be *durable* so that it can be stored away or saved.

There are not many materials that fulfil these four requirements and that can therefore be used to make coins. Metals have proved the most suitable. Certain shells, too, have been used as money.

People are prepared to work and sell their products for money not because money in itself is of any use to them, but because they are confident that other people will be willing to provide goods or services for the money they receive. Money is universally accepted because it is universally accepted. Here we have another self-confirming expectation. Since people expect others to accept the money, they are prepared to accept it themselves. The actual utility value of the material of which it is made scarcely has any relevance. Modern societies increasingly use paper money, and more and more people have banker's cards with electronic IDs. 'Plastic' can be used to obtain banknotes, which can then be exchanged for gold at the 'central bank' that issues banknotes on the state's instructions. As long as this conversion is perfectly possible, almost no one bothers to do it; then again, if everyone were to try to convert their money into gold, it would no longer work, as there is not enough gold in stock to exchange for all the banknotes. However, even if the money can no longer be exchanged for gold, even if it is just made of paper, even if it is no more than an electronic code, it still works well as a medium of exchange, as long as everyone is confident that it can be passed on to someone else in exchange for useful goods and services.

3 Market formation

When the supply of a product equals the demand for it, the market for that product is in equilibrium. If demand outstrips supply, prices will rise. Rising prices means that fewer people will want to purchase the product, as they cannot afford it. Meanwhile, the number of people willing to sell at this higher price will increase, as they anticipate receiving more money for their goods. Once prices have risen by a certain amount, demand and supply will even out again. Where prices fall, the reverse trend occurs: demand increases while supply declines. In this way, the play of supply and demand, or the *price mechanism*, reaches an equilibrium. At a certain price, demand and supply are exactly equal.

In a *free market* there is *perfect competition*. No one buyer or seller controls enough of the market to influence the price individually. In reality, the market often works very differently. A large number of small coffee growers will find themselves pitted against a few major wholesale buyers, who agree a purchasing price among themselves. Or a single international concern (the market leader) may produce the lion's share of heavy trucks, enabling it to control the sales price. So fair competition presupposes a large measure of social equality between those participating in the market, whereas in actual fact the relations are often asymmetrical. In extreme cases the supply or demand may be completely dominated by a single party – a *monopolist*. Even then, however, the monopolist is still dependent on the other party, the sellers or purchasers as a group, although each one of them is far more dependent on the monopolist than the other way around. The balance of power is tipped to one side.

The remarkable thing about a 'free' market is that no one is in charge, and yet the market forces exert a compelling force on buyers and sellers alike. Although no one imposes the price, no one can change it either. Those who offer less than the going price will be unable to buy, while those who want more than the market price will be unable to sell (they will 'price themselves out of the market'). Offering more than the market price means incurring higher costs than the competition, and asking for less generally means accepting a loss. So the price mechanism is an instance of social coercion, but one without a coercive agency.

As a rule, markets arise unintentionally and without any planning. They can function without anyone being able to survey and understand them in their entirety. Market formation is a textbook example of a blind process.

Market formation can only take place when there is a fair measure of pacification – when consignments transported to and from market are not raided by thieves and when trade does not degenerate into fist fights and robberies. For the market to develop further, laws and law enforcement are essential; since every exchange is also an agreement, there must be rules for deliveries and payment. Disputes must be settled through the courts, and rulings enforced where necessary. A good monitoring system is essential to prevent coins being counterfeited or filed down, paper money being forged or electronic accounts being tampered with. All these tasks are the responsibility of the state. As will become clear, market formation, city formation and state formation are all closely connected.

A market is a junction of exchange relations – it is where supply meets demand. This obviously happens at actual meeting-places like street markets, where greengrocers' stalls are set up in a row and purchasers go to do their shopping. The stock market works in much the same way, but the dealing is in shares instead of vegetables. An auction is a market at which each lot in turn is offered to a group of buyers. Market squares are traditional meeting-places, and inns, craftsmen's workshops and trading offices tend to cluster around them. They are also often the initial nucleus of a town – signalling the beginning of city formation. Even today, street markets and shopping streets (another type of market) are still primarily found in city centres.

Then there are markets without any geographical location, that are 'everywhere and nowhere'. The best example is the 'labour market'. It is not located in any particular place, but it is everywhere where there is a supply of labour and a demand for it. The market mechanism works here too, since people in one place are generally aware of the wages obtainable elsewhere.

The market mechanism is an interplay of expectations among interdependent people. When demand for a particular article outstrips supply at that time, it soon sells out. Alternatively, the price is raised, until a number of purchasers drop out, who are unwilling to buy at that higher price. Once producers notice that their product is selling well or that prices are rising, they increase production in the expectation of boosting sales and increasing profits.

Sometimes this price mechanism goes completely haywire. When the demand for computers increases, the demand for computer chips increases accordingly, and chips therefore become more expensive. The manufacturer responds by expanding production. After all, a heavy demand will mean a large turnover and attractive profits. Expansion means buying new machines and more factory space, and training new technicians, so another year passes before chip production has really been stepped up. Meanwhile, however, other manufacturers have also been expanding. As a result, chips are now in such abundant supply that they are no longer so easy to sell. Now the manufacturers have to lower the price and are forced to accept a loss. Several companies go bankrupt, while others decide to close factory buildings they have only just built. Meanwhile, with prices at a new low, all sorts of applications are dreamt up for these chips that would otherwise have been much too expensive. The demand for chips increases again, just when supply has taken a downward turn. Prices soar more than ever and manufacturers expand their operations yet again. This time, factories are even built by newcomers on the market hoping to take advantage of the higher prices. A little later it turns out that supply is again exceeding demand, even more than before. Prices are slashed, and bankruptcies follow in quick succession. Until the next time around. It is a series of self-denying expectations with ever more dramatic swings. This process is sometimes referred to as the 'hog cycle', because the pig market is the classic example.

Manufacturers caught up in this process could agree among themselves to limit production. This would enable them to keep prices high in spite of a limited turnover. However, one producer could ignore the agreement and step up production while prices were still high, thus obtaining an additional turnover and higher profits. The other manufacturers would not let the rogue profiteer get away with this and they too would increase production. Prices would slump after all, and everyone would end up making a loss. This has a familiar ring to it. It is another example of a dilemma of collective action. In some cases, the collaboration proves sustainable. Producers commit themselves to an agreement in a *cartel*, or it is the state that enforces the limitation of production. In fishing, cattle breeding and agriculture, binding production quotas and price control measures are particularly common.

4 Expansion of the money economy

Market formation is in the first place the formation of an exchange network – the lengthening and strengthening of exchange relations. More people exchange more goods more often, and over a greater distance. In the second place, market formation is closely related to the process of *monetarization* – that is, the gradual elimination of barter trade and the introduction of a general medium of exchange and payment – *money*. Similarly, labour is no longer rewarded with a meal and a bed for the night, or with a share in the produce, but is paid in money, in *wages*. In modern societies almost all goods and services can be expressed in terms of their value in money – 'everything has a price'. This is the hallmark of a *money economy*. Monetarization has already reached an advanced stage of development, and the process is still going on.

In individual households, money does not generally change hands when family members perform domestic tasks. This work is unpaid. But when women have jobs outside the home they have less time to take care of the children and to shop, cook, clean the house and wash and iron the family's clothes. Sometimes men make more time to share in these tasks. Often, however, the small children are taken to a day nursery, which expects to be paid in money. TV dinners are purchased from the supermarket, or the family eats out or orders pizzas and pays the bill. Much of the work that was once done largely by 'housewives' free of charge is now done by outsiders, for a price. The extra money needed to pay for all these services is earned by the two partners in their jobs. All this amounts to a monetarization of domestic affairs.

Money has a bad reputation. 'All people think of these days is money', someone will sigh. Indeed, since money can buy almost anything that can be done or made – almost anything for which we are dependent on others – it is hardly surprising that it has come to loom so large in people's lives. Yet societies not dominated by money nonetheless know envy, greed and meanness. There, people will strive to acquire even more land, or even more cows.

Market formation, the division of labour and monetarization have dramatically changed human life, the nature of society. A modern society such as the Netherlands or the UK is the result of these processes, which have by no means come to an end.

5 Economic and other social relations

Economic exchange relations are usually embedded in other social ties. The corner grocer eventually becomes a good acquaintance whose shop continues to be patronized by the neighbourhood, even if he charges 60p more for a kilo of cheese than the supermarket. But at the corner shop people exchange local gossip, the shopkeeper may set certain items aside for regular customers, allow goods to be bought on credit, have a bone for the dog and sweets for the children, arrange to have shopping delivered, and serve the occasional stressed customer after hours. Providing credit, in particular, was an important role of shopkeepers in working-class areas not so long ago (and still is in developing countries). Nonetheless, small shopkeepers have gradually lost more and more ground to chain stores.

Among friends and acquaintances, money matters are approached with extreme caution. Even in today's free market society, it is considered improper in many circles, between friends and relatives, to make a profit on a transaction, ask for interest on a loan, or expect to be paid for lending a helping hand. Instead, the loan, chore or item supplied is regarded as a kindness, to be repaid not in money but with a similar friendly turn at some time in the future. In people's memories there is an item left outstanding, an unpaid debt. So an exchange relationship does exist, in the widest sense of the term, but recompense takes the form of social favours instead of payment in money.

On the other hand, blood relationships may provide a strong foundation for the expansion of trade networks. People who belong to the same family or clan tend to trust each other more than outsiders. Any abuse of trust would soon become known in that circle and could lead to the culprit being ostracized by the rest.

Even global trade networks often connect only a small number of agents trading in the same product. In a branch of this kind, everyone knows everyone else. Swindling will precipitate a swift loss of reputation and possibly expulsion from the club. Doctors and lawyers too gradually build up their professional reputations, and their comments in turn help to determine the regard in which their peers are held. These peers will tend to refer clients to those who have a good reputation among fellow professionals. In much the same way, brand names provide products with a reputation. The more widely known and respected the brand name, the likelier consumers are to choose it.

Economic relations are also relationships of trust. This often makes them exclusive. Anyone who is unknown in a particular branch will be viewed with suspicion and may be excluded. This means that the advantages to be gained in that network are confined to a small circle of *insiders*. So this mutual trust also has the function of warding off potential rivals and restricting competition. Entire sections of the population are often simply excluded in advance. This is an instance of *blanket discrimination* – that is, the exclusion of a category of people from a particular social position on grounds that are irrelevant to the qualities needed to fill it. Economic life generally proceeds without violence. But deliveries and payments are sometimes enforced with threats and displays of force. For instance, entrepreneurs may be forced to pay for protection from arson or plundering by the 'protectors' themselves. This is known as a *protection racket*. In principle, however, conflicts are solved on the basis of rules of law, and if necessary by the courts. A court order can be enforced by the police. Dispensing justice and maintaining law and order are hence indispensable conditions for economic traffic, and it is up to the state to ensure that these conditions are met.

10

How People Cooperate on the Basis of Rules and Instructions: Organization

Every day thousands of trains transport millions of passengers between hundreds of stations. The system usually works well, but if a train is delayed, travellers become annoyed. This is understandable, since now they risk missing their appointments and hence inconveniencing others. Passengers apparently take it for granted that their trains will run on time. But why should they expect it? An individual traveller may wonder why that particular train, of all trains, had to be late, but in general the opposite question is far more interesting: how do all those trains generally manage to run on time? How can such an endlessly complex timetable work at all?

Clearly, the mechanism that underlies the market would not work with the railways: engine drivers or conductors cannot be left to choose a suitable time of departure and destination, nor would this result in anything like a serviceable schedule. It may work in the marketplace, but here it would lead to total chaos and cause terrible accidents. A different mechanism altogether operates in the case of the railways – that of *organization*.

Engine drivers keep as closely as possible to the railway timetable. This timetable has been drawn up by planners in minute detail long beforehand. All times and destinations are determined precisely. The staff working the trains are expected to keep to the schedule and to the other rules and regulations, and to follow the instructions of their bosses. These bosses also have to work according to the rules, and do as instructed by their own superiors, right up to the most senior director.

Every organization has its rules, its managers and its subordinates, and there is a well-defined division of labour in which everyone's duties are set down in detail. Each organization also has a specific purpose – to transport passengers and freight by train, for instance.

An organization is a system of people and resources, geared towards performing a particular task. There are countless organizations in society, and everyone has to do with many of them on an everyday basis. Some organizations are very old. The Catholic Church, for instance, has existed for almost two thousand years. Military organizations such as armies arose even earlier. But the twentieth century in particular witnessed a huge growth in the number of organizations in society. Moreover, they have greatly increased in size and complexity. So although they have their historical forerunners, organizations are above all characteristic of present-day societies.

These days everyone belongs to some association or other. They too have their rules ('statutes'), and a board presided over by a chairperson, and each sets out to achieve a particular goal. Everyone also has to do with organizations of another kind – business enterprises. The vast majority of the working population are employed by commercial companies – economic organizations. A large company is presided over by a board of commissioners, representing the shareholders who each own a small portion of it. Day-to-day management is in the hands of a board of directors. Again, there are regulations. A company is an organization set up to make a profit by making certain products or supplying certain services.

Political life too is dominated by organizations. A political party is an association that puts forward candidates for election and tries to exert influence through elected members of parliament to achieve the aims of its programme. The biggest organization of all is the state. The state apparatus is a collection of all sorts of administrative organizations, such as ministries and agencies, led by the government. Very large, complex and highly regulated organizations are known as *bureaucracies*. These occur chiefly in the state machinery, but large companies and associations are also often bureaucratic in nature.

1 Organizations as social arrangements

Schools are textbook examples of organizations. Each one will have its own management, led by a head teacher, supervised by a board of governors or a local authority. An inspectorate attached to the education ministry monitors the way the school functions and checks that statutory rules are kept to. The school will often have its own house regulations as well, and the head will ensure that teachers and pupils keep to them. Within the school, there is a detailed division of tasks. There are teachers for each class, and at secondary school for each different subject, as well as a caretaker, secretaries, and so on. Teachers are expected to follow the instructions of school management. However, the management cannot decree as it sees fit, but also has rules to keep to, and can only compel teaching staff to do or refrain from certain specific things. In class, pupils must do as their teachers say, yet teachers have only limited authority over them; they have little say in what pupils do in their leisure hours, and their control over pupils' clothing or hairstyles differs from one school to another – and indeed from one country to another.

Any modern organization will have people occupying senior and subordinate positions, but the relationship of authority between them is limited in terms of time, place and subject matter. Even the most highly regulated of organizations has its twilight zones – areas in which bosses' authority over their subordinates is controversial. For instance, should school governors have any say in the private lives of teachers working in the school? Should a director have the authority to forbid employees to join a union?

The work of a school is largely geared towards preparing pupils for their school-leaving examinations. This is the primary and most visible task of a school organization – its *manifest function*. But like all organizations schools also have *latent* or hidden functions: for instance, they free parents from caring for their small children for part of the day, and keep teenagers out of the labour market for a few more years – a function that is particularly relevant in times of unemployment.

A latent function of many associations is to create opportunities for their members to socialize while they collaborate to achieve the manifest task of their organization. And a hidden function of many government agencies is to provide employment.

The roles in a modern organization are formal in nature. They are laid down in writing, and in principle they are impartial and provide for all eventualities. Impartiality means that no exception may be made for the geography teacher's son or a 'good-looking' pupil; the same rules apply to everyone. Relations between superiors and subordinates and the division of tasks are also set down in formal rules.

Even so, all sorts of ties evolve in organizations alongside these formal relations, and sometimes diametrically opposed to them. *Informal relations* of this kind are not laid down anywhere, and are seldom discussed openly. They are different in each case and often highly personal. In companies where people work for a piece rate – in other words, they are paid per item produced – the fastest workers will often work below their capacity. They do not want it to be obvious how much they could really produce, as this might bring the piece rate down; nor do they want to make things too difficult for their slower fellow workers, who would otherwise earn far less than themselves.

Schools too have their informal relations. Cheating is strictly forbidden, but there is also a strict informal rule that pupils should not 'tell' on each other, and it may be regarded as 'mean' to make it impossible for a fellow pupil to see your work. According to formal relations, the best pupil in the class should enjoy the highest esteem, but in informal relations the most popular is often the 'toughest' or the 'prettiest' pupil. Among themselves, pupils have very different concerns, and build up informal relationships based on friendship or love, as well as rivalries and enmities.

2 Organization and stratification

All people are consumers, and when they purchase something for their own use, they do so on the consumer market. The suppliers of these items are mostly commercial companies, such as chain stores, department stores, car dealers or clothes manufacturers.

Most adults are also employees, and the vast majority work within organizations, such as government agencies or commercial companies. They generally have someone working above them, and sometimes they have people working under them. They work at set times, on well-defined tasks, and receive a fixed salary. People in high positions can arrange their work at times to suit themselves, and have their own offices where no one can enter without knocking. Lower down the scale, tasks are assigned from hour to hour, sometimes even from minute to minute, or a boss will tell employees exactly what to do. There is always a supervisor who may pass by at any moment. While senior company officials can decide how best to do their work, lower-ranking employees are often assigned limited tasks, and so can never complete anything entirely on their own. This also means that they feel less committed to the end product.

In modern societies, relatively few people work for themselves – as 'self-employed' farmers, shopkeepers, craftsmen, doctors, lawyers or architects, operating largely alone, with the assistance of relatives or a few employees. Once the business becomes larger, and more staff are taken on, they generally have little time for their original work. Eventually they become full-time managers, and their little firm turns into an organization, an enterprise.

Only a few generations ago, a far larger proportion of the population had businesses of their own. And when people did take employment, it was generally in one of these small firms. Large enterprises did not arise until the invention of steam power, which enabled dozens of machines to be operated at once. Spinners, weavers and other manual workers could not compete with mass production lines, and lost their source of income. The new factories took on workers to operate the machines for a wage. That was the first *industrial revolution*. The advent of chemical fertilizers, improved crops and farming machinery made it possible to produce far more food with far fewer people, forcing many who would formerly have been farm labourers to seek work in the factories. They too became dependent on wages.

As enterprises became larger, there was a need for better bookkeeping and more supervision within the organization. All sorts of intermediate positions were created, in between bosses and workers. These accountants and middle-management staff wore 'white collars' and were clearly differentiated from the 'blue-collar' workers in the assembly lines. They generally had more schooling and were trained in bookkeeping, commercial correspondence, foreign languages and so on. Although not self-employed – and therefore different from shopkeepers and farmers – they were also distinguished from industrialists on the one hand and the workers on the other. They became an intermediate layer – the *middle classes*.

A second revolution occurred in industry with the introduction of electricity as a source of energy for machines and the internal combustion engine to drive vehicles. And we are still in the throes of a third one right now – *computerization*. The primary emphasis is now no longer on strength and on speeding up production, but on processing information.

Once again, all sorts of tasks are being taken over by machines – computers and robots – which are able to do complex work very accurately and fast. And once again many workers are being made redundant. This time, even tasks previously carried out by the middle echelons and highly skilled workers are being computerized. Accounting and clerical work is now largely done with the aid of specially designed software. Robots are being used to replace workers, for instance in assembling and painting motor vehicles.

The past fifty years have seen a substantial increase in the number of women in paid employment in the industrial world. The influx of mothers into the workforce has increased the demand for day nurseries, domestic help, ready-to-eat dishes, restaurant meals and home-delivered dinners. Conversely, where all these things are readily available, mothers will be more likely to seek paid employment.

In ages gone by, children's careers were largely determined by the capital their parents had managed to amass to seek 'good matches' for their daughters and to set their sons up in the family business. But today middle-class people rarely have their own businesses, and are seldom able to build up a sizeable capital. Their way of offering children good opportunities is to ensure that they have as much education as possible. The level at which people are appointed within an organization largely depends on the amount of education they have had. Someone who has no educational qualifications will be given a simple job to do, without any prospect of promotion. Someone with a university degree, on the other hand, will be appointed straight to the middle ranks, and may go on to reach one of the most senior positions.

The level at which you leave the 'education organization' determines where you will end up in the 'labour organization'. This position determines your income and standing, and hence the place you will live and the kind of holidays you will have, it determines your pattern of spending on the consumer market and the kind of education you will seek for your own children.

The sharp dividing lines between shabby paupers without jobs, propertyless labourers, a lower-middle class of self-employed people and an upper echelon of propertied classes have become a little blurred in modern society. The transition from one layer in the stratification to another has become more fluid. People who are without jobs and possessions are eligible for benefit – another provision processed by a bureaucratic organization. Because of this, their pattern of spending and their lifestyles are less sharply delineated from those of other people than in the past. The distinction between manual and office workers has also become blurred, now that a great deal of heavy, dirty work has disappeared, while employees in factory halls and offices sit at monitors and operate keyboards.

Property is distributed a little more evenly over the population than in the past. Much of it now belongs to pension funds and insurance companies, which administer it to pay pensions and benefit to those who are insured, when they are no longer able or expected to work. The most senior officials in an enterprise are no longer the owners, but are employed by the company, while the ownership of the enterprise is split into shares and divided among a larger number of shareholders. Instead of a building with separate floors, modern society has therefore come to look more like a staircase with countless small steps, each of which is only a few inches higher than the one below. Even so, the difference between the highest and lowest steps is still very great. And people's position in the labour organization determines where they stand on this social staircase.

Market relations and relations within organizations are specific and impersonal. They are about buying and selling, or quality of work measured against the level of pay. Emotional responses – whether people like each other, any personal hopes or expectations they may have concerning one another – are left out of consideration altogether. It is also increasingly unimportant what people's origins are, what religion they profess, whether they are men or women and what sort of lifestyle they have adopted. However, as already noted, that is the formal façade. Behind it there are informal relations in which all these differences often have a definite emotional impact. For each of their needs people turn to different organizations. To borrow a mathematical term, one might say that they are 'resolved into factors' – each factor relating to a particular organization – but the interdependence between these different needs is entirely ignored. As 'human beings' people are reliant on themselves, their families and the circle of friends they are able to build up and sustain. The sense of belonging that was once taken for granted in extended families, in guilds, villages, neighbourhoods and religious communities has all but disappeared – along with the stifling atmosphere that often went along with it. Nowadays people have to exert themselves to find and preserve something of that community life in the small circle of their relatives and friends, in clubs and sometimes at work. This is why a society with a high level of organization is more likely to foster social isolation and loneliness.

11

How People Form States and States Form People: State Formation and State Intervention

Even people who scarcely take an interest in sport can be found suddenly cheering for 'their' national side against a team from another country. And in the other country people glued to TV sets will be cheering just as loudly for their own national side.

People evidently feel a strong connection with the country they live in, a feeling that comes out most clearly when there is some competition with another country. On holiday abroad you may catch yourself defending your compatriots if someone says something unfriendly about them, whereas in your own country and among people of your own nationality you will often be far more critical. No one takes kindly to criticism from an outsider. It is only when you are 'outside' that you notice what you feel 'inside'.

In sport all this is fairly innocent; rivalry there may be, but it is regulated rivalry, played strictly according to the competition rules. There may be a 'fight', but it will be fought largely with sporting means and seldom with real violence. Even so, an international sporting event is a kind of repeat of the violent history of national states, though here they enter the arena in a purely symbolic sense.

A glance at the atlas reveals that the whole planet, with the exception of Antarctica and the oceans, is divided into states with clear frontiers. This is a fairly recent development. Not so long ago there were wide open spaces that were not really under anyone's control or where groups were constantly battling for supremacy. Sometimes one band of warriors would succeed in subjecting all its opponents in a large territory – it would acquire sole 'dominion' over that region. After a while other conflicts would erupt, either with rebels inside the territory or with rivals in a neighbouring district. Even today, numerous regions of the world are plagued by armed power struggles.

1 State formation and increases in scale

Whoever owns something has something to lose and something to defend. Peasant societies live under the constant threat of armed gangs that may suddenly descend to plunder and loot at will. If the villages are destroyed and all the peasants slain, there will be nothing left to plunder the following year. But if the warriors exercise self-restraint, a more balanced triangular relationship will develop in the course of time. The warrior gang will offer to protect the peasant village from other similar gangs, and in return it will receive from the peasants a fixed tribute, or tax, which will leave them with just enough to survive.

This is the essence of the process of state formation: armed gangs protect producers from warriors, including themselves, and appropriate the producers' surplus – that is, their yield over and above what they need to survive. Protection and taxation go together. The more land comes under the rule of a warrior gang, the more tax can be collected, the larger and stronger will be the army the ruler maintains to fight other rulers and to expand his territory, and the larger the surplus yield he will be able to appropriate. The spiral will continue to widen, unless rival warrior gangs manage to check this expansionist drive.

Industrial societies are more productive still and hence more vulnerable. Again, armed states offer protection from other states and levy taxes in their own territory. The task of suppressing acts of violence within the territory is delegated to the police, while defence against external violence – that is, from other states – is the army's task.

In most Western societies, the state's activities have increasingly been restricted by the passage of legislation and by court rulings. Rulers are designated in elections. And even the most austere fiscal regime will leave taxpayers a good deal more than the bare minimum needed for survival.

Modern societies with their nuclear plants, chemical factories, airports and electronic networks are the most productive in history, but they are also immensely vulnerable to sabotage, presenting attractive opportunities for terrorists.

In Europe and Asia, the process of state formation also meant gradual increases in scale. Warriors succeeded in expanding their territories by defeating their rivals, thus acquiring a stronger power base. But each territory would fall apart again after a while: heirs would carve it up or rebels would break away and set up for themselves. In the end, one prince would manage to secure a pivotal position: the others would then have to join ranks to oppose this prince or vie with one another for his support – in any conflict, the party protected by the prince would prevail. In these circumstances, the *free competition* would become a *monopolist competition* to obtain the support of the dominant prince. For his part, the prince would be able to play the smaller rivals off against each other, and eventually subject each of them in turn. In this way a larger sphere of influence would arise, which might collapse again in the face of a united opposition or if plagued by internal divisions.

In the course of history, units formed to attack and defend a territory became larger and larger, as new military and administrative techniques made it possible to operate effectively over larger distances. Even in ancient times vast empires were formed, but their rulers had far less power over their subjects than the governments of modern states have over their citizens. In the space of about 5,000 years, the scale on which it is possible to exercise power effectively has expanded from a village of a few hundred souls to today's superpowers, with territories populated by hundreds of millions of people. And while one superpower – the Soviet Union – has fallen apart, another – the European Union – is in the making.

During the Cold War (1948–89), the world had two rival superpowers. All the other countries competed for the support of one of these two, but they could also play the two off against each other, and this gave smaller powers a certain leverage. Since the collapse of the Soviet Union, the competition has centred on gaining the support of the one remaining superpower. The United States has become a monopolist: any alliance able to gain its support has the edge over its opponents.

In any power structure, what matters is how skilfully rulers exploit their opportunities. It is not enough for them to be decisive generals and bold commanders – they also have to be shrewd diplomats, able to placate or intimidate their opponents as the occasion demands, or to employ a 'divide and rule' strategy.

In any battle, victory will depend partly on the size of an army and the soldiers' courage, military skill, determination and unity of purpose, and partly on the level of arms technology and military organization. Horsemen in suits of armour could soon gain the upper hand over a peasant army wielding nothing more threatening than clubs, spears and bows and arrows. But once armed with pikes, crossbows and muskets, foot soldiers came into their own against mounted troops. The arms race has been with us for a very long time.

At least as important as weaponry is an army's organization, for in the heat of battle there is a real risk of widespread panic and total chaos. A general who is able to deploy troops in a strategic order of battle and to maintain discipline among the ranks can prevail over far larger but less disciplined armies. Particularly in battle, control and self-control – 'self-direction' – are absolutely vital. That is why military culture is geared towards strengthening morale and inculcating discipline in every soldier. In modern warfare, physical strength and agility are becoming less important than accuracy in operating complicated weapon systems and reliability in performing long-range assignments, far below sea level or high in the sky, and very far from the human enemies who are to be killed. Every general must ensure that troops in action are supplied with food and clean drinking water and are properly armed; otherwise the campaign will be lost through hunger, disease or a lack of ammunition. The longer an army's supply lines, the more it is 'out on a limb'. Provisioning and communication become more difficult and the army is forced to plunder the lands it passes through or make the supreme effort needed to haul its supplies across great distances. Modern production techniques, vehicles and communication systems allow huge armies to advance for thousands of miles, increasing the potential scale of warfare to cover the entire planet.

In the Second World War, fighting power turned out not to be the crucial factor; victory hinged on the industrial apparatus that had to keep that fighting power operational. In this respect, the United States proved to have a decisive advantage. Since then, having an economic and technological edge has become even more important.

In conflicts, warring parties are under a strong compulsion to apply any means that will improve their own odds. Fighting techniques and modes of organization that give one side an advantage are adopted as fast as possible by the other side. If this proves impossible, the other side will find it is fighting – and losing – an 'unequal battle'. If states fight each other over a long period of time, they end up resembling each other. In this regard too, states are formed by and against other states.

2 The legitimation of power

Mere force of arms, even when accompanied by organization, discipline and diplomacy, will not suffice to maintain control over a territory in the long term. The subjects who are obliged to pay taxes and to do military service are more likely to accept these obligations if they are convinced it is all in a good cause, that the ruler has a clear right to rule, that the ruler's power is lawful and *legitimate*; authority is legitimate power.

A ruler who has prevailed over the enemy can point to this victory as proof not only of outstanding skill, but also of supernatural support – in a word, the conqueror can claim to have been divinely chosen. This generates *charisma* – the special attraction that leaders have for their followers – and becomes the basis on which the position of power is justified, the foundation of authority. Rulers will often use religion to legitimize their rule. A king may claim divine descent, invoke divine inspiration or guidance, and find sources that seem to suggest that his reign was foretold by prophets or in holy scriptures. His successors have only to point to their descent from the charismatic founder and their unbroken line. *Tradition* is another vehicle for *legitimizing* positions of power. Customs that have been passed down since time immemorial are considered legitimate on the sole grounds of long usage.

Authority can derive legitimation from yet a third source – the *procedures* for designating a ruler and for the exercise of this rule. There are rules for hereditary succession and for the election of leaders. These leaders are in turn under an obligation to keep to certain rules in performing their tasks. The procedures are enshrined in written statutes, which are themselves promulgated in accordance with rules enshrined in a country's constitution.

State formation is the establishment of an effective and legitimate monopoly on force and taxation within a certain territory. A state is formed in competition with other states in adjoining territories.

3 Nation formation

The people who live together within a particular state develop increasingly close mutual ties and in most cases eventually constitute a single nation. The formation of a nation is the consolidation of similarities among people within a territory and the accentuation of their differences with those outside. Nations too are formed by and against other nations. If this national awareness becomes the one guiding principle, it is called *nationalism*.

Nowadays, national allegiance is generally stronger than an allegiance to a particular region or city, village or neighbourhood, enterprise, society or even religious community. Only family ties are stronger. In wartime, people – especially young men – are prepared to kill people of other nations and risk their own lives for the sake of their own nation.

In modern states, education is the most important means of consolidating national unity and passing it on to later generations. At primary school, children learn everything they need to be able to live together with the other inhabitants of their territory. For instance, they are taught a uniform language with fixed spelling rules and a standard pronunciation and grammar, even if they speak a regional or local dialect at home – or the language of another country, from which they themselves or their parents originate.

A *nation state* is a state in which the inhabitants regard themselves as belonging to the same nation. Nation states are typical of Western Europe; examples include France, Spain, the Netherlands and the United Kingdom. But even these countries contain groups that have long stood out from the majority and that have often sought more independence or closer ties with a neighbouring country. This applies to the Basque people, to the Catalans and Alsatians, to the Frisians, and to the Scots, the Northern Irish and the Welsh. In fact, a complete identity of nation and state exists nowhere; in all countries there are differences of language, religion and origin within a single people. Human diversity has increased still further over the centuries through *migration* – movements of people from one area or country to another. And even more migrants are on the move in today's world.

Hence states and nations are not formed in completely parallel processes; furthermore, various nations may coexist within a single *multinational state*, such as India or the former Soviet Union. This is often a heritage of *colonialism*. A foreign power established its rule over areas inhabited by peoples with different languages, religions, origins and historical backgrounds. Later on, when the colony became independent, these diverse peoples would continue to live within the single state formed by the colonial power, without constituting a nation in all respects. Furthermore, sometimes one people would be dominated by several powers, so that even after independence it would come under separate states. This happened not only in Africa, but also in Europe, where the Germans were divided in the wake of their defeat in 1945 into two states until the reunification of 1990 brought them under a single state once more.

The boundaries of a state and a nation do not always coincide. Within a particular territory there may be groups that speak different languages, profess different religions, come from different countries and look different, or who lived under a different state not so long ago. These characteristics frequently go together, reinforcing the differences. In some cases, however, these differences exist and yet count for little. Much has changed since the 1950s, when the gap between Dutch Protestants and Catholics was still so wide that each denomination had its own clubs, trade unions and political parties, and mixed marriages were quite rare. This is almost unimaginable today. Even these divisions, however, did not undermine the unity of the Dutch nation. No group wanted to break away from the state; there was no organized violence between groups, nor was there any large-scale disobedience to the state of the Netherlands.

The people who live in the 'Low Countries' do not share a common faith. The region is split by language barriers between speakers of French, Dutch and Luxemburgish, and it is divided into three different states – the Netherlands, Belgium and Luxembourg. The Balkans are divided in similar ways, but unlike the Balkans, the Low Countries have preserved peace for centuries. Apparently, differences in language, religion or origin need not lead to war. Violent conflict is most likely to erupt when recollections of recent armed struggles are kept alive; the dormant hatred and mutual mistrust can easily be rekindled.

When a state collapses, for instance because of changes in the international balance of power, its citizens also lose the protection it provided. This happened when the European powers were driven out of their colonies in Asia and Africa, and it happened in Eastern Europe after the collapse of the Soviet Union. In the resulting vacuum, domestic peace and security are no longer assured, and one group may sense such a potent threat from another that it closes ranks, organizes and procures arms. This group may now in turn threaten the initial antagonists, who respond by uniting even more firmly than before and taking up arms. People who had never even defined themselves in terms of a group before now suddenly find themselves compelled to join one of the parties for their own safety. The divisions become increasingly sharp and violent, and the bloodshed continues until new states form, which together maintain a balance of power.

4 Areas and limits of state intervention

The state intervenes in many areas of society. Both the defence of a country and the maintenance of law and order – external and internal security – have traditionally been a matter for the state. With its police and criminal justice system, the state exercises its monopoly on violence. In so doing it is bound by the laws of the land; the state has the legitimate power to apply force as a last resort.

The primary responsibilities of a state are related to the

provision of collective goods. But state intervention differs from voluntary collective action, in that collective goods are funded from taxes that a state can levy compulsorily. State coercion bypasses the notorious dilemma of collective action. Traditional duties of the state hence include the building and maintenance of roads, railways and harbours. Public health care and social security, as well as education, are also among the responsibilities of a modern state, which is known for this reason as a *welfare state*. Long before the state concerned itself directly with caring for the poor and sick, there were local voluntary and collective *care arrangements*. It was often the prosperous, established citizenry who set up these arrangements. The presence of the poor in their midst was detrimental and dangerous for them too – poverty led to crime, rebellion and disease. In other words, there were *external effects* associated with poverty, consequences for those who were not directly affected. The rich could not contain these external effects by acting individually. Collective action was called for, for instance by devising systems of poor relief or hospitals for the needy. In this case too, any wealthy citizens who had not contributed to the plan would nevertheless profit from the diminished threat of violence and disease; the familiar dilemma of collective action applied here as elsewhere.

Government intervention could resolve this dilemma. In the nineteenth century, city councils in particular made provision for the poor in the industrial towns, which helped to allay the threat of revolts and epidemics. In the twentieth century, care arrangements such as social insurance were imposed compulsorily by the state on a national scale. With the support of progressive entrepreneurs, moderate trade unionists and resolute regimes, these provisions, which initially met with resistance from the self-employed, were gradually put in place. The extremely rapid expansion of the welfare state after the Second World War slowed down in the 1980s and 1990s. Some elements were transferred to private insurance schemes; some types of benefit were reduced to cut expenditure and to adjust wage costs to cope with the international competition provided by the new industrial countries.

In today's societies the state takes on a wide range of other concerns: traffic, housing, the arts, the environment and agriculture. It gives grants and levies taxes on all sorts of economic activities. Basically you can hardly make a move these days without encountering the regulations or agencies of the state. The final stage in state formation is the extension of state intervention – the state's increasing involvement with every aspect of life in society. And in spite of efforts to reverse this process, or at least to slow it down, for instance by *privatization* – the sale of state-owned property and the contracting out of state responsibilities to private individuals – it is still continuing.

However wide-ranging state intervention may be, it is subject to many restrictions. In the first place, the state's actions are restricted by legislation. In a state governed by the *rule of law*, there are statutory provisions that must be observed even by those in positions of the highest authority, intended to protect citizens from the power of the state. In the second place, many states are *parliamentary democracies*. This means that the highest power is exercised by members of parliament chosen by the electorate, which nowadays includes all adult citizens.

The enormous expansion of state intervention in people's lives creates its own limits. Decision-making and policy implementation have become so complicated and unfathomable that many measures have effects quite different from those foreseen – or sometimes fail to have any effect at all. Retrenchment or employment policies, tax regulations and anti-drugs campaigns supply copious examples.

The existence of other states also helps to define the limits of a state's power, just as it defines its geographical frontiers. While it is true that in principle all states have sovereignty and recognize no higher power, in reality they must take account of each other, and their power is increasingly constrained by supranational organizations such as the United Nations or the European Union. States are also increasingly subject to international law. But there is not yet a monopoly on the legitimate and effective use of force on a global scale.

5 Power, the majority and democratic feedback

A modern state apparatus is a collection of large organizations, government bureaucracies employing millions of officials, including civil servants and employees of state-run enterprises and agencies. This state conglomerate is divided into ministries, each of which is led by a minister – the executive machinery that is responsible for performing the state's business. Taxes are imposed, collective goods are provided, from public health care and education to the maintenance of law and order and the defence of the country. The *government* consists of parliament and cabinet, generally headed by a prime minister; some countries have a president as government leader.

The state apparatus may be pictured as a gigantic hierarchical network with the head of government at the top, surrounded by ministers in key positions. It branches out from senior civil servants down to the rank and file of bureaucracy. At the tips of the branches are individual members of the public, who are connected to the government bureaucracies in many ways (for instance as students, grant recipients, taxpayers, benefit recipients, road users, rail passengers, hospital patients, pensioners and so on).

But built into this structure is a vast system of *democratic feedback*. All adult citizens have the right to elect members of parliament, and in republics such as France and the United States they can also elect the president.

The United Kingdom and the Netherlands are examples of *parliamentary monarchies*. The head of state is the monarch, but a cabinet of government ministers rules the country, and for its mandate to rule, the cabinet must have the support of a majority in the elected lower house of parliament. In such parliamentary democracies, democratic feedback allows the majority of the electorate to have the final say. But how do such majorities come into existence? The most important factor is the distribution of opinions and preferences among the electorate. Can these preferences be graded on a sliding scale from 'less' to 'more'? Many can be – for instance, all opinions that could be translated into a preference for more state intervention ('left-wing') or a more *laissez-faire* approach to the economy ('right-wing'). Other opinions could be graded on a sliding scale from 'nationalism' to 'internationalism' in foreign policy. Here too, right-wing and left-wing tendencies may be distinguished to a certain extent, roughly parallel to that in the first scale. Certain parallels are also discernible with a third scale, ranging from 'conservatism' to 'progressiveness' in questions of morality and religion.

These dimensions in public opinion change in the course of time. In Western democracies the 'third dimension', that of morality, looms largest in questions relating to death (e.g. euthanasia, abortion) and sexuality (e.g. homosexuality in the armed forces, child sex abuse). A fourth dimension has also come into its own in recent times. This is *environmentalism*, the care for the natural surroundings as opposed to a blanket preference for economic growth (*productivism*). Once again a rough correspondence is discernible with the leftist and rightist preferences in the other dimensions (although environmental protection is 'conservative', it also requires powerful state intervention in the free market and a willingness to make national sacrifices for the benefit of the global environment – choices that are of 'leftist' appeal).

On each of the four political scales that have been mentioned, we may distinguish three positions, roughly speaking: left-wing, right-wing and the centre ground. A quick sum teaches us that this generates a total of eighty-one (3^4) different combinations. But there is no need for eighty-one different political parties. Elections are seldom about all these dimensions at once. Anyway, not all conceivable combinations of positions would actually be found among the electorate. A party wishing to do well in an election will draw up a programme including a combination of positions likely to attract a large proportion of voters. Out of the original eighty-one combinations, we might be left with, say, twelve actually formulated in party programmes; these twelve political parties, each with its own coherent programme, would provide a good 'scale model' of the political diversity of the electorate. But this would not create a parliamentary majority that could support a cabinet in parliament or pass legislation. The variety of opinions among the electorate eventually has to be reduced still further, into two camps – government versus opposition.

There are two alternative solutions to this problem. The first is the *constituency system*, in which a country is divided into a large number of electoral districts or constituencies. The candidate who gains most votes in a particular district is elected to represent it in parliament. To win an election, therefore, it is essential to draft a programme beforehand that will attract most votes, given the preferences among the electorate. In practice, this means that only two or three national parties will be left at national level, and that the voters will be forced to choose between these two or three available parties. A vote for one of these parties will actually increase that party's chances of coming to power.

The second solution is to have candidates elected for the entire country instead of each representing one constituency. This is the *proportional representation system*. All candidates who gain more votes than a certain quota (the total electorate divided by the number of seats in parliament) are elected. There is no reason for candidates to make compromises beforehand. The twelve most important options are represented by just as many parties with their candidates (the Netherlands has sometimes had more than twenty political parties!) and people can each cast their votes for a party that stands for a combination of opinions approximating their own. What this means, however, is that eight, ten or even all twelve of these parties end up in parliament. It is only after the election that negotiations can begin with a view to forming a majority coalition. The consultations among the party leaders can result in very different coalitions

– left-wing, right-wing, or in the centre ground. The electorate can no longer exert any control on this process. In a constituency voting system, the results of the election decide who is to be in power until the next election, whereas under proportional representation everything hinges on the negotiations conducted afterwards.

In many elections, one set of preferences – often the socioeconomic dimension – takes precedence over the rest. This simplifies the problem of the *aggregation of preferences* – that is, the combination of opinions needed to make up a majority programme. For in this case, all that counts is where the electorate stands on this one, relevant scale. But how are the public's views distributed in this dimension, and above all: how strong is the centre ground? If a large number of voters hold views in the centre, and very few incline to the extremes, each party will draw up a programme that tends towards this centre ground. After all, there are few votes to be gained by advocating an extreme position. A *unimodal* distribution of this kind, represented by a bell-shaped curve, will foster moderation and compromise. But if the electorate is sharply divided, with few people occupying the centre ground and large numbers favouring radical positions on either side – a *bimodal* distribution represented by a curve with two peaks – parties will avoid the centre ground and each incline to one of the extremes, where the votes are to be found. This obviously makes it more difficult to form any kind of coalition afterwards, if this proves necessary. If there is a bimodal distribution in all dimensions, and all the voters who are 'right-wing' in one dimension are also 'right-wing' in the others, the electorate is divided into two irreconcilable camps: *coinciding divisions* reinforce one another. But if the peaks occur in different places in different dimensions – if those who favour international cooperation are fiercely divided on economic issues, and if the voters who are conservative in questions of morality disagree violently on the environment – the constellation becomes more difficult to grasp. Eventually a compromise can be achieved by exchanging concessions. In this case there are *cross-cutting divisions*, which do not reinforce one another.

Sometimes a minority can get its way by insisting on a point of principle that is of minor importance to the other parties and giving way on a different issue on which its views are more flexible. This is the strategy of the *intense minority*. Religious parties have sometimes prevailed against the majority view by making concessions to other parties on socio-economic issues they consider non-essential in return for concessions on religious matters.

Unimodal distributions and crossing lines lead to compromise and stability. Bimodal distributions and coinciding lines promote conflict and tend to produce wide swings in election results.

Parties are kept to the principles defined in their programme by their members, who have joined for the sake of these principles and hold the party leadership to them. But at election time parties seek out the centre ground (in the case of a unimodal distribution of preferences among the electorate) or move closer to the nearest extreme (in the case of a bimodal distribution). In a constituency system, there will often be a period of radicalization after an election. The militant members want to see their support rewarded by the party taking a clear stand on certain issues. In a proportional representation system, on the other hand, this is a phase of negotiation, concession and compromise, in which a majority coalition is formed. The centre parties have an advantage in this process. It scarcely matters how many seats they have gained. They can move in either direction to seek coalition partners, and best of all is to have partners on both sides, which they can play off against one another from their ideal strategic position. The parties at either end of the scale, on the other hand, prefer to form the smallest possible majority coalition, as any addition will move the government programme away from their points of view and force them to make further concessions.

Politicians are not only in the business of formulating

positions that will attract a majority of votes; they also do their best, of course, to change voters' views. This is the second element in the feedback system – the political feedback from politicians and opinion leaders. The radicalization of public opinion (a shift towards a bimodal distribution), the activation of a particular dimension of preferences, or an appeal to solidarity and the willingness to compromise, all belong to the arsenal of strategies with which political leaders can try to change the political landscape (the distribution of preferences among the electorate) and increase their own chances of coming to power. All kinds of resources, from political propaganda to personal powers of persuasion, are deployed to achieve this. Nowadays a politician's image is a collective product, designed by a team of propaganda specialists and promoted in newspapers and on radio and television. But advertisements for one candidate will always have to contend with those of rivals. And politicians never have the field to themselves. Within certain statutory limitations, people may see, watch and listen to what they want, say what they want to anyone they please and meet and cooperate with anyone they please. These political freedoms are anchored in the – written or unwritten – constitution. States are forbidden to forbid their citizens to influence each other's opinions. It is on the basis of these opinions that people elect those who govern them.

12

Globalization: Towards a Worldwide Society?

Do all the people in the world together make up a worldwide society? That depends on whether those people are actually connected and interdependent. This chapter will look at global interdependencies and the conditions for the existence of a world society. The discussion will range from production and distribution to internal and external security (which coincide at global level), solidarity and orientation, and finally, to problems of interdependence in a worldwide context.

1 The global economy

There is a global economic system. Thousands of years ago, caravans crossed the steppes and deserts of Asia. Later, ships sailed the Mediterranean and the Indian Ocean, laden with precious goods from remote corners of the earth. In the seventeenth century, Amsterdam was a centre of trade in grain, timber and furs from Eastern Europe, spices, silk and jade from Asia, and silver and gold from the New World. The new prosperity in the growing towns generated a great demand for articles that were either unavailable in the immediate surroundings or were better made or produced more cheaply in other regions. Spanish and English wool went to Leiden or Antwerp to be woven and dyed. In America, cotton and sugar were grown on huge plantations for export to Europe. And arms and printed cotton fabrics were shipped by British traders from America to Africa, where they were exchanged for slaves, who were deported to the American plantations on a large scale.

With the industrial revolution, the demand for imports from distant parts rapidly increased. Steam-powered looms could process whole shipments of cotton imported from the south of the United States. The colonization of large parts of Africa and Asia brought new products to Europe. From Africa came palm oil, which was made into margarine, rubber from the East Indies was used in transmission belts and tyres, and dried bird manure from South America made excellent fertilizer. Tea, coffee, cocoa, peanuts and coconuts were shipped to Europe and the United States, initially in fast sailing ships and later in steamships, while manufactured articles from Europe were exported to Africa.

Britain, France, and in the twentieth century the United States, were at the heart of this global economic system. It was there that the banks and mercantile houses had their headquarters, and it was to these regions that raw materials were imported from all corners of the world to be processed industrially into finished products which were then exported to all continents. Africa, Asia and South America were the peripheral areas in this system. There, mining and agriculture yielded the raw materials that were traded, shipped and processed by entrepreneurs in Western Europe and the United States, and it was they who made the profits. Even after the colonial powers were forced to retreat and independent states were proclaimed in Asia and Africa, these continents for the most part remained the marginal areas of the global economy. Japan and Canada, followed a little later by Hong Kong, South Korea, Taiwan and Australia, developed into economic centres that now belong to the nucleus of the global economy. Several countries occupy intermediate positions: they include India, Indonesia, Brazil and China. But particularly in Africa, many countries are still exclusively producers of raw materials, without any industry or banking system of their own. The oil-producing countries occupy a special position. They have managed to accumulate tremendous wealth, even though they only provide raw materials, of which there is a finite supply.

One major problem for the marginal economic regions is that industrialization occurred earlier in other parts of the world. The core countries, that already possess industrial plants, expertise, connections and experience, are constantly ahead of the periphery in economic competition. This is why many people from underdeveloped countries go to the core countries to study and work, and why businesspeople there invest in promising ventures in the economically developed regions. This is a constant drain on marginal countries' human talent and financial capital. They have to take out loans and pay huge sums in interest to the economically developed countries. To be able to export, the marginal regions have to focus on the mass cultivation of one or a handful of products for the global market – sugar, cotton, coffee, tea, coconuts, tropical timber and so forth. This *monoculture* – growing a single crop – makes their economies very vulnerable to any dip in the price of their export product on the global market.

Clearly, the peoples of the world are very closely connected with one another in the global economic system, but their mutual dependence does not amount to economic equality. It is an asymmetrical dependence. A sizeable proportion of the earth's population is scarcely included in the world economy. The few remaining nomadic peoples are still almost entirely outside it, as are the hundreds of millions of small farmers who largely provide for their own needs, have almost no money income and can therefore acquire very little from elsewhere.

Development aid can only have a modest corrective impact on the inequality between core and marginal areas. Of more potential importance are the efforts being made through international economic organizations to regulate the global markets for raw materials and to stabilize prices. If rich countries were to abolish import duties on products from the developing world they could provide a powerful boost to production and exports in those countries.

2 Global politics

There is also a global political system, which is of course intimately entwined with the global economy. Just as the world economic system connects people through markets and enterprises, the world political system links them primarily through states. Each state has a monopoly on force and taxation within its own territory, but there is as yet no world state that could impose taxes on people throughout the planet and maintain law and order by force when necessary. States are to a large extent free to act within their own borders. In their relations with one another, states are bound by rules of international law. The United Nations Security Council may also remind them of these rules. But there is no permanent police force that can enforce compliance with them. Taking action against a country that has violated international law is feasible only if a powerful nation such as the United States, backed up by allies and sanctioned by the United Nations, decides to intervene. But this is worlds away from an impartial police force that would have the same kind of powers as those of domestic police forces in countries governed by the rule of law.

States come into existence through violent competition. The relations formed in such struggles also constitute a system of mutual dependence, but not one of mutual coordination. The first large-scale efforts to bring extensive territories with a multiplicity of peoples and a large number of rulers under a single coordinating authority took place after 1000 BC, with the founding of the Chinese Empire, the empire of Alexander the Great and the Roman Empire. World empires of this kind set up a very wide-ranging but very thin network of power relations throughout the conquered areas. The subjected rulers were laid under tribute; they had to pay regular contributions to the conqueror and could be required to support him in a time of war, but the enormous distances involved made any more active government from the centre impossible.

After the collapse of the Roman Empire it was not until the end of the fifteenth century that imperialism arose again in Europe. Along the coastlines of Africa, Asia and the Americas, trading posts were set up, each fortified by a small garrison and surrounded by a small colony of merchants. The various governments of Europe first set out from these posts to impose trading conditions that were as favourable as possible to themselves, and later used these strongholds as operational bases from which to undertake military campaigns, culminating in the conquest of the Americas, Africa, and ultimately large parts of Asia.

These colonial empires may have spanned the globe, but they were very thin power networks. It was not until the nineteenth century that colonialism moved into a new, more intense phase of existence. Mining and plantation culture expanded, trade became more important, the machinery of government branched out, and schools were founded on a large scale, initially for each country's elite and later for the rest of the population.

After the Second World War, sustaining the effort of political colonization proved too arduous a task for the European colonial powers. Western ideas of freedom, equality and national identity were adopted by the colonized nations and turned against the Western rulers themselves. A few years later, almost the whole of Asia was liberated. Around 1960 most African countries gained their independence. The former colonial powers, and France and Britain in particular, were able to maintain economic relations – and to a far lesser extent political ties – with their former colonies. Although the heyday of colonialism had lasted a mere sixty years, the colonized peoples were incorporated for once and all into the global economy and the world political system. After independence, the young states joined international organizations and through the mass media they became involved in a global commercial culture. Millions migrated from the marginal regions to the capital cities of the West.

The two world wars hastened world integration – not

merely because war itself is a form of interdependence. Back in the First World War, the United States became involved in the European theatre of war, battles were fought over the German colonies in Africa and Asia, while soldiers from the French and British colonies fought in Europe and the Middle East. The Second World War was fought throughout Europe, in South Asia, and in East Asia, which was initially under Japanese occupation. After the First World War the League of Nations was set up as a consultative body where disputes between nations could be resolved, and after the Second World War the United Nations was founded, with even more far-reaching powers.

After 1945 the world became divided into two power blocks – the United States with its allies as opposed to the Soviet Union with its vassals; that is, the capitalist democracies versus the 'people's democracies' of state socialism. In the polarizing world of the Cold War, both sides integrated at an accelerated pace into military alliances coupled with political alliances and separate trading zones. But the Western avant-garde art and commercial entertainment industries were not reflected by any alternative, communist culture. Still, the East–West opposition was fought out symbolically by the sportsmen and sportswomen who competed at the Olympic Games.

This period came to an end with the collapse of the Soviet Union, which dragged the rest of the communist world with it in a process of disintegration. But in the longer term the net result may yet prove to be more cohesion in the global system, if the coordination between East and West is expanded.

The enormous destructive power of nuclear weapons in today's world is a menace to all the inhabitants of the planet. This global hazard also increases the interdependence among peoples and their states. The consciousness of a common threat has helped to form safety regimes for nuclear (and chemical and biological) weapons, involving inspections and the destruction of these 'non-conventional' arms, as well as non-proliferation agreements.

The expansion of the global economy has also increased states' reliance on each other. In times of recession many states try to protect employment in their own countries by banning imports, so that consumers will be compelled to buy products manufactured at home. This is called *protectionism* in international trade. But if countries take protectionist measures, the exports of their trading partners are brought to a halt. These countries stop receiving foreign currency that they could use to import goods from elsewhere, and this rebounds on the protectionist countries by limiting their exports. Global trade shrinks and unemployment rises everywhere. A worldwide economic crisis, such as happened in the years 1929–36, is the result.

Protectionism suppresses free trade in the global economy; in times of economic decline it is in the short-term interests of each individual state to take measures to limit exports, unless all states coordinate their policies and agree to allow free trade. Here we may recognize a dilemma of collective action – this time among states. In recent years the conclusion of several agreements has expanded free trade in large parts of the world.

The European Union is based on a binding agreement among the member states to remove all obstacles to mutual trade and the movement of persons and capital by establishing a 'free trade zone'. This has been an arduous process, and conflicts still flare up from time to time.

In the global political system that has started to take shape since the end of the Cold War, the United States plays a leading role. It does not have a global monopoly on force, but there is no state or coalition of states that could defeat it, and without the United States, no alliance can prevail. So global politics is now in a state of *monopolist competition*, in which almost all states compete for the support of the greatest power, the United States.

3 Global cultural system

There is as yet little sign of any worldwide sense of 'us'. Yet between states, there are weaker and stronger affinities. Democratic states have seldom fought one another, and in a crisis they have often rushed to one another's assistance. For instance, in both the world wars of the twentieth century, Britain and the United States supported France.

Is there a sense of identity shared by all human beings? The world religions suggest that we are all 'God's children'. But this universal message has not been able to prevent bitter religious wars, nor has it led to a generalized sense of solidarity, even in peacetime. Modern science, and biology in particular, emphasize that humanity is a single species of which any female could in principle mate with any male and produce fertile offspring.

The havoc wrought by two world wars and above all the threat of nuclear war, its potential consequences still more devastating, has widened and strengthened the realization that world peace is in the interest of all peoples. Still, this awareness has not made humanity into a single community, united in a sense of solidarity. Human beings do not have a common enemy against which they could take concerted action. The formation of any group always involves exclusion, but no one can be excluded from humanity. This is why the universal sense of 'us' is still nebulous and poorly developed, and why it is generally subordinated to national sentiments among the members of a people, to the sense of togetherness that binds believers in the same faith, or to the solidarity that exists among the citizens of a state.

Still, certain current developments are strengthening the realization that it is a question of 'one world or none at all'. These include new modes of communication and transport, and a stronger sense of interdependence in areas such as environment and migration.

In the space of a human lifetime there has been a revolution in communications technology. Radio, telephone and television, computers and satellites ensure that people are now far better informed – and informed far more rapidly – of what is happening in the world about them than in the past. These days it is not unusual for viewers to watch a missile striking a target thousands of miles away, at the very same moment, and to see the panic and devastation it causes. Viewers can scarcely shut themselves off from the images of famine, flood and epidemic being beamed from the other side of the world. They also know that they can help – in principle, at any rate, and to a small extent. Nor can they deny that the distant strangers are suffering just as much as they would themselves from these calamities, since documentaries and correspondents' reports have familiarized them with the everyday lives of their fellow human beings elsewhere.

Meanwhile, the villagers of India and Africa are also watching life in other parts of the world. They too have radios, and see films and television images. People know more about one another than in the past, and are more conscious of the ways in which they are connected to other people. This fulfils one of the requirements for greater solidarity, but for this feeling to develop further, more is needed. The revolution in mass communication and the expansion of global trade also mean that people are growing more alike. They increasingly enjoy the same entertainment, and they are increasingly purchasing the same sort of consumer goods.

For centuries there has been a 'high' culture of classical art forms, admired by educated people both in and outside Western countries. Other civilizations too have their centuries-old 'high' cultural traditions. Popular art forms, the culture of less highly educated people, tended to be regional. Through the electronic media, a mass culture has developed worldwide, with particular appeal to young people. The popular music of African-Americans – blues and jazz – has mushroomed into all kinds of popular music: rhythm and blues, rock and roll, rap, house and so on. Musicians in other regions have taken to combining their own traditional music with this popular 'world music', creating genres such as reggae, soka and rai – hybrid forms that have become popular throughout the world. Popular music is rebellious, sensual and cosmopolitan youth entertainment; it is already a kind of world culture, with the United States as its heartland. But there are other centres of mass culture in the world. India, for instance, has its own vast popular entertainment industry. Films full of music and dancing are distributed from India throughout large parts of Asia, but receive scant attention in the West.

Dress codes among young people also point to the dissemination of a global mass culture. Jeans, T-shirts and trainers are popular all over the world. There is nothing odd about seeing demonstrators clad in jeans and basketball shoes shouting anti-American slogans in some distant land. This is also related to the expansion of world trade, of course – these products are transported to all corners of the earth. Motor vehicles, refrigerators and TV sets can be found everywhere and look the same everywhere, and people everywhere learn how to use them in the same way.

People travel more frequently and further afield than in the past. Europeans who would scarcely have taken any kind of holiday fifty years ago, and who would have taken small trips in their own country thirty years ago, now travel by car, caravan, train or plane to the sun-drenched Mediterranean, and in recent years they have started going even further afield, to Egypt, Thailand or Australia. Although such tourists have little contact with the local population, they nonetheless become more familiar with foreign customs, other languages and above all with new culinary experiences. Immigrants from these countries seize the opportunity to open exotic restaurants in Europe, giving city-dwellers a choice of dishes from all over the world.

A global culture is in the making, primarily for young people and primarily in tourism, sports, entertainment, music, dance and clothing. Patterns of consumption are also growing more and more closely related. In a nutshell, there is an increasing diversity of supply in more and more places; and yet this diversified supply is gradually becoming more and more similar from one place to the next. This is a consequence of expanding world trade, the growth of air transport and the revolution in the mass media.

4 Interdependencies: the environment

If there is one problem that clearly confronts humanity as a whole, it is environmental pollution. The contamination of rivers and seas, air pollution from fumes generated by industry and traffic, the depletion of the ozone layer and the acidification of forests do not respect national frontiers. Discharges in Switzerland contaminate drinking water in the Netherlands, exhaust fumes from German traffic harm Norwegian woods, a nuclear disaster in the Soviet Union can jeopardize harvests throughout Europe, and soot generated by oil burning in Kuwait turns up in Hawaii.

It is precisely this transnational character of environmental problems that makes them more difficult to solve. If the Italians were the only ones to suffer from their own waste and emissions, and if they experienced no ill effects from the pollution emanating from other countries, they could solve the problems in their own country, and coercive measures introduced by the Italian state would suffice. But the inhabitants of one state also suffer from the pollution caused by those of another state, over which they have no control. Once again, there is no world state that could impose a global environmental law on all the world's inhabitants.

Every country could begin by reducing the pollution within its own territory as much as possible, including emissions and discharges that have an even worse impact on the population of other countries than on its own – in the hope that other countries will be just as well-intentioned. But if this becomes expensive and requires considerable effort, if it drives up production prices compared to those of the country's competitors, such an enlightened policy will meet with resistance. Here again we encounter the familiar dilemmas of collective action. If one state limits pollution without others following suit, it will be a costly exercise while doing little to improve the global environment – and therefore not even do much to improve the air, soil and water within the state's own borders. But if no state is prepared to do anything to curb pollution, environmental degradation will steadily worsen, with major repercussions for all countries.

Since it is a fact of life that states have a large measure of sovereignty, the only solution is to set up consultations among states on limiting pollution. This will eventually boost confidence in the willingness of other states to play their part in environmental conservation, and increase the willingness of each individual state to participate. A free press can make a useful contribution here. If officials know that polluting practices will lead to an environmental scandal and arouse indignation both at home and abroad, they will make more of an effort to protect the environment. Concern for the environment did not start with politicians, civil servants or entrepreneurs, but with nature lovers and scientists who succeeded in generating debate in the media and mobilizing public opinion. In democratic countries the next stage came when the electorate started to vote for politicians who promised to turn the tide of environmental degradation, provided it would not have too damaging an impact on profits and employment.

These democracies are among the most prosperous countries, whose industries cause a large part of the pollution and which are better able to bear the costs of environmental conservation. The less prosperous countries in marginal areas contribute less to environmental degradation and are less able to bear the costs of environmental conservation. The 'core countries' also have an interest in protecting the environment in marginal areas, but if one of them contributes to the costs involved, the other countries will profit without it costing them anything – and yet another dilemma of collective action raises its head.

5 Interdependencies: migration

Each year tens of millions of people throughout the world journey from countryside to towns, from provincial towns to capital cities, and from marginal areas to metropolises in core countries. Some are fleeing from violence in their homelands, others are eager to gain an education, but the vast majority are looking for jobs. There is nothing new about these migrations, but they are greatly on the increase. Travelling has become easier and cheaper. People see more images of distant countries and may well fantasize about their prospects there. But the main reason for migration is poverty and unemployment in the regions of origin.

It is not the poorest and neediest members of society that tend to migrate, but the people who can pay for a journey and who have relatives or acquaintances in the country of their destination – in other words they tend to be enterprising, healthy, young people.

The prosperous Western countries are increasingly closing their doors to fresh waves of immigrants. This policy is only partly successful. In a country governed by the rule of law, police checks are never wholly adequate, and besides, there is always a need for cheap labour, hired illegally if need be. The pressure of immigration on the world's major economic powers is first and foremost a result of the enormous prosperity gap. For these countries, the flows of migrants are an external effect of the poverty in the marginal regions of the world system. They are a consequence of the interdependence between the affluent world of the West and the poor regions in the periphery.

Tens of millions of people still die in these countries as a result of malnutrition or diseases that can be cured elsewhere by a simple remedy. About half of the people who are alive today have never learnt to read, and the majority of the world's population do not have running water or domestic sewerage systems. Furthermore, poor hygiene and inadequate health care in poor countries are bringing back diseases that were once contained, such as tuberculosis and malaria, in new and more dangerous strains.

Daunting though these problems may be, they could be solved with the technical, organizational and financial resources that are available today. The problem lies elsewhere: who should bear the costs and make the necessary effort? Again, it comes down to a problem of distribution and coordination.

The people who live in the affluent world of the West are more conscious today than in the past of the misery in which so many lives are lived in the marginal regions. As newspaper readers and TV viewers they are constantly confronted with it, often in a compelling way, but as individuals there is little they can do about it. So while their sympathies are deeply engaged, they feel powerless to help. This leads to feelings of indignation, but also to a sense of resignation and indifference. Similar emotional responses were seen in the nineteenth century, when the inhabitants of the industrial cities were confronted with the wretched lives of the factory proletariat, which at the time seemed completely unavoidable. In the twentieth century, a social security system was built up in the industrial democracies, which eradicated the worst consequences of poverty. It also produced a different mentality, *social awareness*: the consciousness that all the members of a society are mutually dependent, and that while no one is individually responsible for someone else's misery, the state can alleviate it by means of a benefit system to which everyone contributes.

No such solution exists for the misery in other countries. Social awareness is far less developed on a global scale than in a national context. Still, Westerners in particular are more inclined to identify with complete strangers in foreign parts than in the past.

Could the prosperous countries conceivably develop a social policy in relation to the destitute peoples inhabiting the world's marginal regions? For this to happen, there would first have to be an awareness among the people in the prosperous countries that it would ultimately be in their own interests to do so. To stem the flow of migrants to the wealthy West, it is essential to increase prosperity in marginal regions, and hence to improve levels of employment there. Increased prosperity is also necessary in order to persuade countries in the economic periphery to do more to protect the environment. Migration and the environment are hence two interests that core countries have in greater prosperity in the periphery – two forms of interdependence that exist between the two parts of the global system. A third area of interdependence relates to global trade. To expand the market for products from the core regions means increasing purchasing power – and hence prosperity – in the marginal regions. It is therefore to the advantage of core countries in the world system to increase prosperity in the periphery. Development aid, investment aid and possibly a transnational social policy could all play a part in this. Once more, the question that arises is whether countries can overcome the dilemmas of collective action in order to forge a common policy. Only then will we have entered a new phase in the development towards a worldwide society.

Further Reading

Most studies in the social sciences are published in English. From the vast literature I have selected a few titles that discuss in greater depth the topics covered in each chapter, and that are particularly readable and interesting.

The first two chapters are so general in scope that almost every social science text contains something relevant. The reader who wishes to consult other introductions to this very wide-ranging subject matter will find a similar approach in *What is Sociology?* (New York: Columbia University Press, 1978) by Norbert Elias (1897–1990), a book that is far more difficult than it appears at first sight, but abounds in interesting and original ideas. Among more recent introductions, *Sociology: A Global Introduction* by John Macionis and Ken Plummer (New York: Prentice-Hall, 1998) can be recommended. More conventional and empirically oriented is the best-selling *Sociology* by Anthony Giddens (3rd edn, Cambridge: Polity, 1999). A most readable introduction from an anthropological point of view is Marvin Harris, *Our Kind, Who We are, Where We Came From, Where We're Going* (New York: Harper & Row, 1989): a 'cultural materialist' overview of the origins, proliferation and social development of the human species.

As already noted, this *Introduction* barely discusses theoretical schools or prominent thinkers. The reader will find excellent presentations of the major schools of thought in C. Wright Mills (1916–62), *The Sociological Imagination* (Harmondsworth: Penguin, 1959) and Johan Goudsblom, *Sociology in the Balance* (Oxford: Blackwell, 1977). A textbook on theoretical schools that has been widely used in recent years is George Ritzer's *Sociological Theory* (New York: McGraw-Hill, 1996). The reader who is eager to learn more about the founders of social science may consult a collection of their writings, such as Ian McIntosh, ed., *Classical Sociological Theory: A Reader* (Edinburgh: Edinburgh University Press, 1997). An excellent secondary discussion of Marx, Weber and Durkheim is Anthony Giddens's *Capitalism and Modern Social Theory*, or the more recent volume edited by Rob Stones, *Key Sociological Thinkers* (Basingstoke: Macmillan, 1998).

The American sociologist Erving Goffman (1922–82) was supreme in his descriptions of people's expectations of one another (chapter 3). In *Stigma: Notes on the Management of Spoiled Identity* (Harmondsworth: Penguin, 1982) he describes what happens when people fail, for whatever reason, to fulfil commonly held expectations. The 'Thomas theorem' that is at the core of this chapter was taken from the American sociologist W. I. Thomas (1863–1947). Edmund H. Volkart edited a collection of his writings: *Social Behavior and Personality: Contributions of W. I. Thomas to Theory and Social Research* (New York: Social Science Research Council, 1951). Robert K. Merton (1910–) described the self-fulfilling and the self-denying prophecies in *Social Theory and Social Structure* (3rd edn, New York: Free Press, 1968).

Max Weber (1864–1920) wrote the classic texts on the stratification of society (chapter 4), published in English in *From Max Weber*, edited by Hans Gerth and C. Wright Mills (Oxford: Oxford University Press, 1946). Another great classic is the essay by Kingsley Davis and Wilbert E. Moore, 'Some principles of stratification' which appeared in the *American Sociological Review* (5, 1945, 242–9). The yearning for prestige is the topic of a book that still makes entertaining reading by the great maverick Thorstein Veblen (1857–1929), *The Theory of the Leisure Class* (1899; New York: Kelley, 1965). A wonderful rendering of American working-class life in the 1960s can be found in Richard Sennett and Jonathan Cobb, *The Hidden Injuries of Class* (New York: Knopf, 1972). Paul Willis vividly describes 'how working-class kids get working-class jobs' in *Learning to Labour* (Farnborough: Saxon House, 1977). The French sociologist Pierre Bourdieu discusses the human urge to achieve distinction, especially through cultural consumption, in *Distinction; A Social Critique of the Judgment of Taste* (London: Routledge & Kegan Paul, 1984). An interesting book on gender relations is *The Longest War: Sex Differences in Perspective*, by Carol Tavris and Carole Offir (New York: Harcourt Brace Jovanovich, 1977). A very instructive and readable book on the relations between newcomers and natives is the study of a neighbourhood in a small English town by Norbert Elias and John J. Scotson, *The Established and the Outsiders* (2nd edn, London: Sage, 1994).

Nancy Chodorow presents an intriguing perspective on socialization (chapter 5) as the social realization of innate possibilities, in her *The Reproduction of Mothering: Psychoanalysis and the Sociology of Gender* (Berkeley: University of California Press, 1978). Another fascinating study of the social control of the affections is Arlie Hochchild, *The Managed Heart; Commercialization of Human Feeling* (Berkeley: University of California Press, 1983). The classic masterpiece by Norbert Elias, *The Civilizing Process* (1939, 1968; rev. edn Oxford: Blackwell, 2000) will prove an entertaining, even engrossing book: however, read the Introduction last. A small book by Stephen Mennell, Eric Jones and Johan Goudsblom, *The Course of Human History: Economic Growth, Social Process, and Civilization* (Armonk, NY: Sharpe (1996) extends this perspective to the development of the entire human species. On recent changes of direction in the civilizing process, see my *The Management of Normality* (London: Routledge, 1990).

Chapter 6 discussed the means of orientation. David Crystal, *The Cambridge Encyclopedia of Language* (Cambridge: Cambridge University Press, 1987) abounds with information, much of which is relevant to the social sciences. Randall Collins, *The Sociology of Philosophies; A Global Theory of Intellectual Change* (Cambridge, Mass.: Belknap Press/Harvard University Press, 1998) breaks new ground by applying sociological ideas to explain the development of philosophy through the ages and across the continents. In an eminently readable study, Bram Kempers, *Painting, Power and Patronage: the Rise of the Professional Artist in the Italian Renaissance* (London: Penguin Books, 1992), reveals the social ties that connect artists and their patrons. The way differences in cultural taste have been shaped in modern society is described for the United States by Lawrence Levine, *Highbrow and Lowbrow; The Emergence of Cultural Hierarchy in America* (Cambridge, Mass.: Harvard University Press, 1988).

Some biologists write about their field with great gusto for a lay audience. The best introduction to 'Neo-Darwinism', one of the topics of chapter 7, was written by Richard Dawkins: *The Selfish Gene* (Oxford: Oxford University Press, 1976). Robert Axelrod, *The Evolution of Cooperation* (New York: Basic Books, 1994) is an account of a brilliant computer experiment on the spread of cooperative attitudes through a population. 'The norm of reciprocity' (1960), by Alvin Gouldner (1920–80), reprinted in *For Sociology* (London: Allan Lane, 1973, pp. 161–78), is a minor classic. The paradoxes of collective action (chapter 8) have been articulated most clearly by Mancur Olsen (1932–88) in his much-cited *The Logic of Collective Action: Public Good and the Theory of Groups* (Cambridge, Mass.: Harvard University Press, 1977). James S. Coleman (1926–95) confronts the problems of collaboration and trust from a related rational choice perspective in his *Foundations of Social Theory* (Cambridge, Mass.: Belknap Press/ Harvard University Press, 1990). How the dilemmas of collective action are overcome in the course of the collectivizing process is the theme of my *In Care of the State; Health Care, Education and Welfare in Europe and the USA in the Modern Era* (Cambridge/ New York: Polity/Oxford University Press, 1988).

The division of labour (chapter 9) is addressed in several classic works, in particular Adam Smith (1723–90), *An Inquiry into the Nature and Causes of the Wealth of Nations* (1776; Harmondsworth: Penguin Classics, 1982), and Emile Durkheim (1858–1917) *The Division of Labour in Society* (1893; London: Macmillan, 1984). A useful collection of essays is Richard Swedberg (ed.), *Explorations in Economic Sociology* (New York: Russell Sage Foundation, 1995). Clifford Geertz, *Peddlers and Princes; Social Change and Economic Modernization in Two Indonesian Towns* (Chicago: University of Chicago Press, 1963) presents an anthropological view of the multiple aspects of 'economic' relations.

Chapter 10 deals with organizations. The fundamental textbook is James March and Herbert A. Simon, *Organizations* (New York/ London: Wiley and Sons/Chapman and Hall, 1958). For a more recent introduction, see W. R. Scott, *Organizations: Rational, Natural and Open Systems* (1981) (4th edn, Englewood Cliffs: Prentice-Hall, 1992). Max Weber and Norbert Elias have written extensively on state formation (chapter 11) in books that have already been cited here. Most instructive is Charles Tilly's *Coercion, Capital and European States AD 990–1990* (Oxford: Blackwell, 1990). More comprehensive still is Michael Mann's *The Sources of Social Power. Volume I: A History of Power from the Beginning to AD 1760; Volume II: The Rise of Classes and Nation-States, 1760–1914* (Cambridge: Cambridge University Press, 1986, 1995). The rapid transformation of states is described by Theda Skocpol in *States and Social Revolutions: A Comparative Analysis of France, Russia and China* (Cambridge: Cambridge University Press, 1979).

The process of globalization (chapter 12) is the subject of many recent publications. A vast historical panorama is depicted by Immanuel Wallerstein, *The Modern World-System. I: Capitalist Agriculture and the Origins of the European World-Economy in the Sixteenth Century; II: Mercantilism and the Consolidation of the European World-Economy, 1600–1750; III: Second Era of Great Expansion of the World Economy, 1730–1840s* (New York: Academic Press, 1974, 1980, 1989). The present state of the world system is discussed in David Landes, *The Wealth and Poverty of Nations: Why Some are so Rich and Some so Poor* (New York: Norton, 1998). Readers who wish to have a convenient overview of the discussion on the globalizing process may consult the collection by David Held et al., *Global Transformations: Politics, Economics and Culture* (Cambridge: Polity, 1999). What it is like to live in this transnational society is perceptively depicted in Ulf Hannerz, *Cultural Complexities: Studies in the Social Organization of Meaning* (New York: Columbia Press, 1992).

Most social science studies appear as articles in reviews. Hence, readers seeking recent material should explore professional journals. The approach of *Theory, Culture and Society* comes closest to this *Introduction*. But that may be a good reason to have a look at other periodicals: *The American Sociological Review* (1936–), *The American Journal of Sociology* (1895–) and *The British Journal of Sociology* (1950–) are widely read, established journals in the field. Readers who are especially interested in statistical time series may consult B. R. Mitchell, *European Historical Statistics 1750–1975* (London: Macmillan Press, 1975) and William Lerner, *Historical Statistics of the United States; Colonial Times to 1970* (Washington, D.C.: Bureau of the Census, 1973).

Index

Index

Index